MEDIEVAL COLORING BOOK

&

REMARKABLE ROMANS COLORING BOOK

2 BOOK BUNDLE

MEDIEVAL
Coloring Book

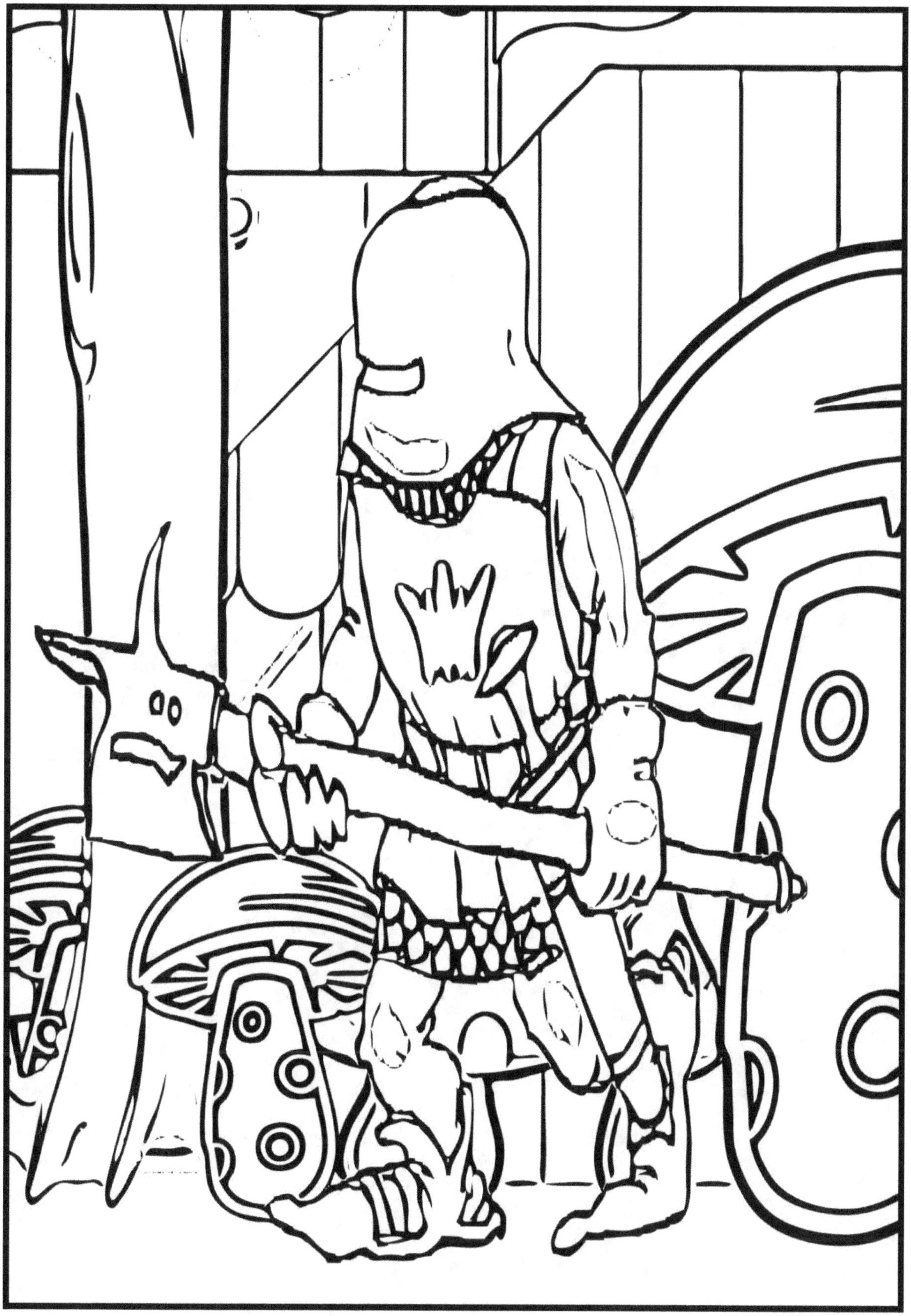

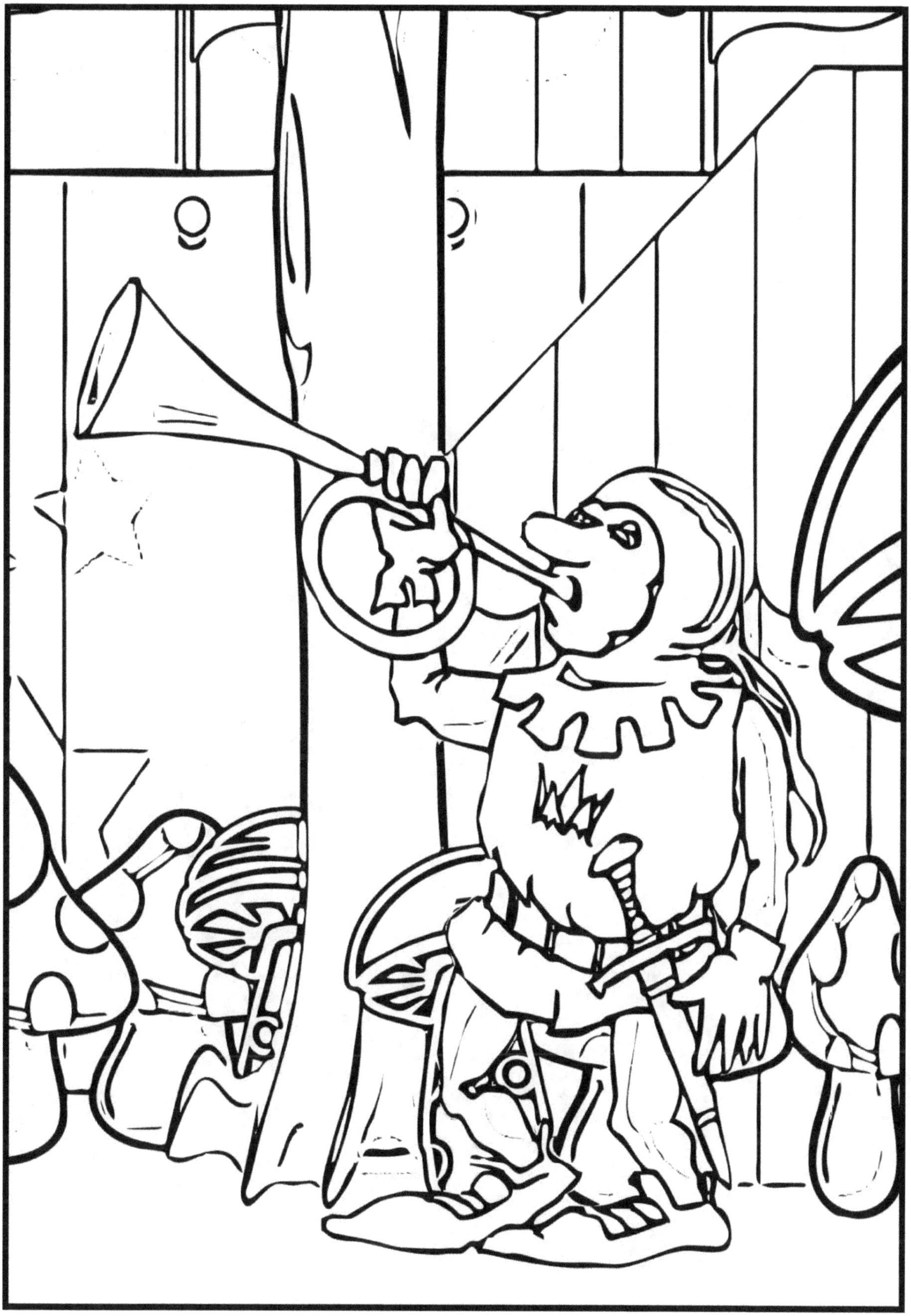

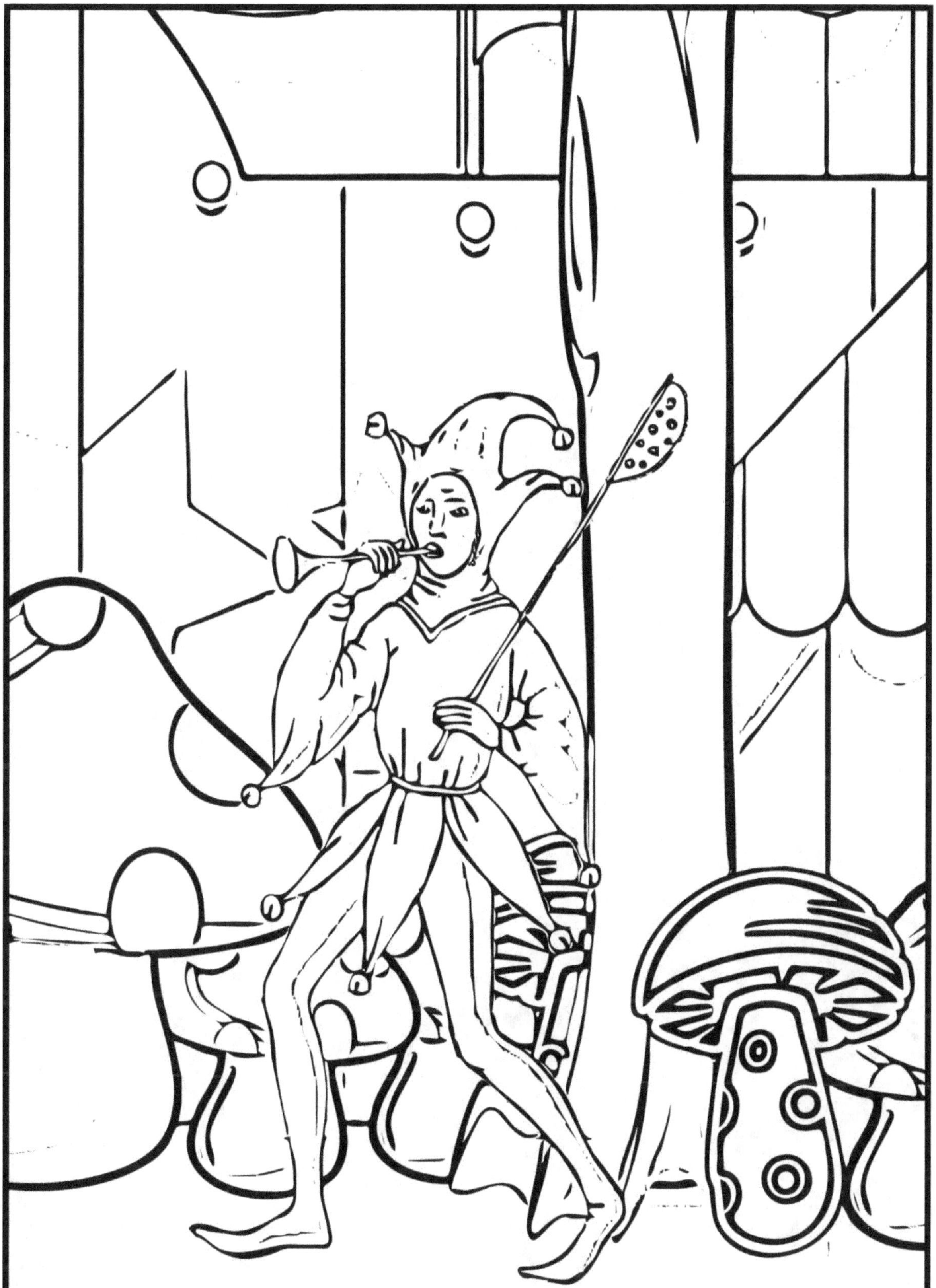

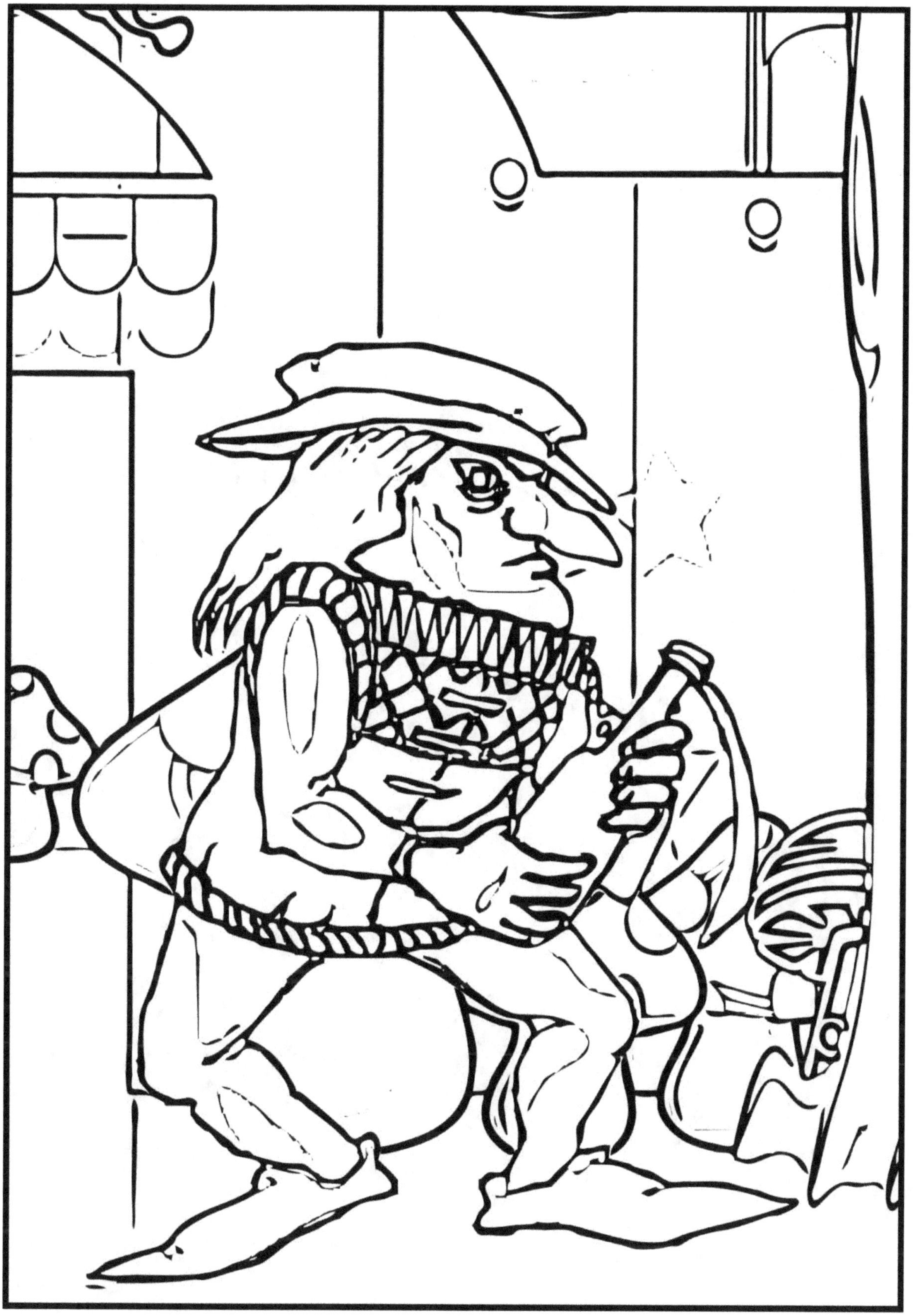

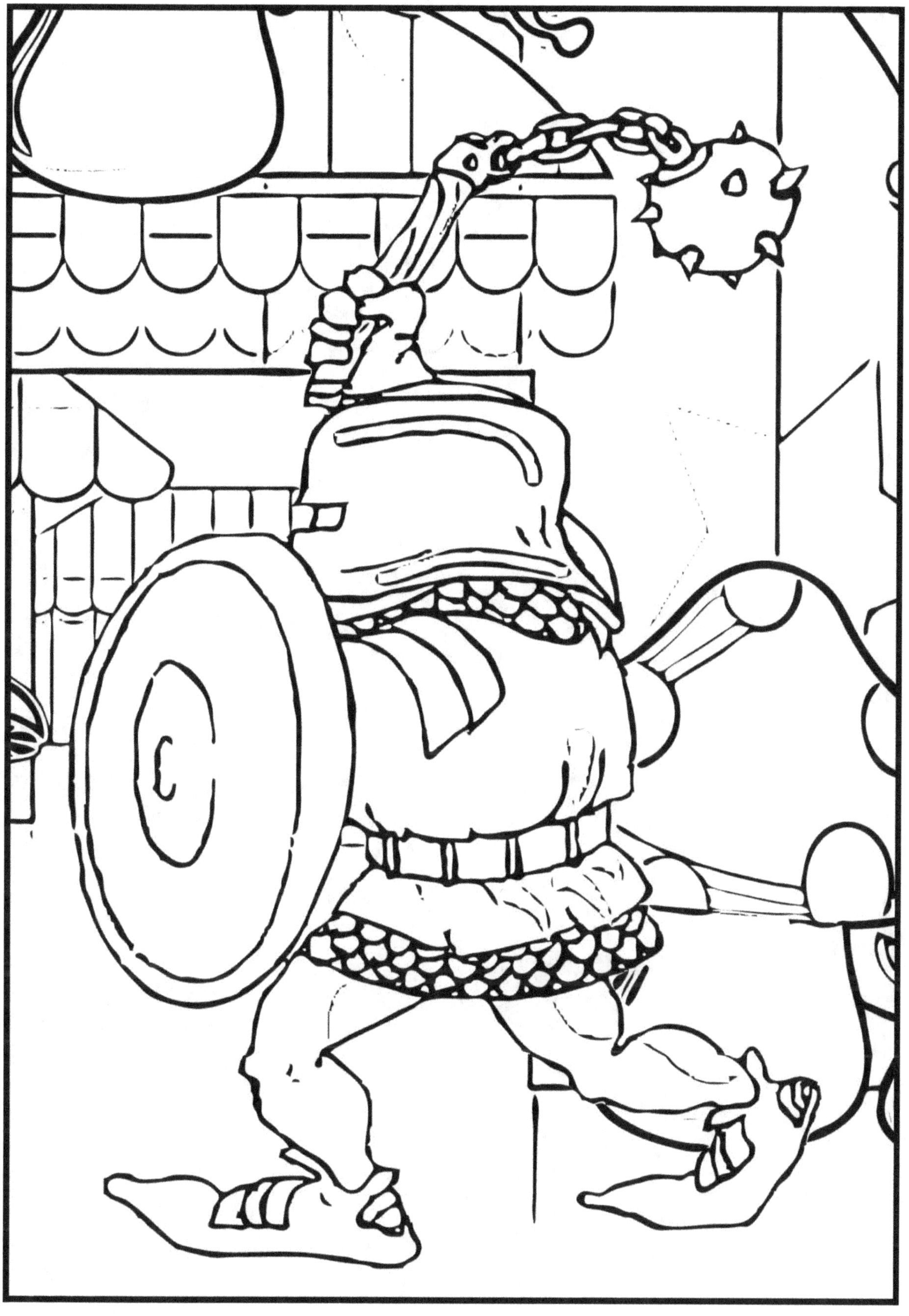

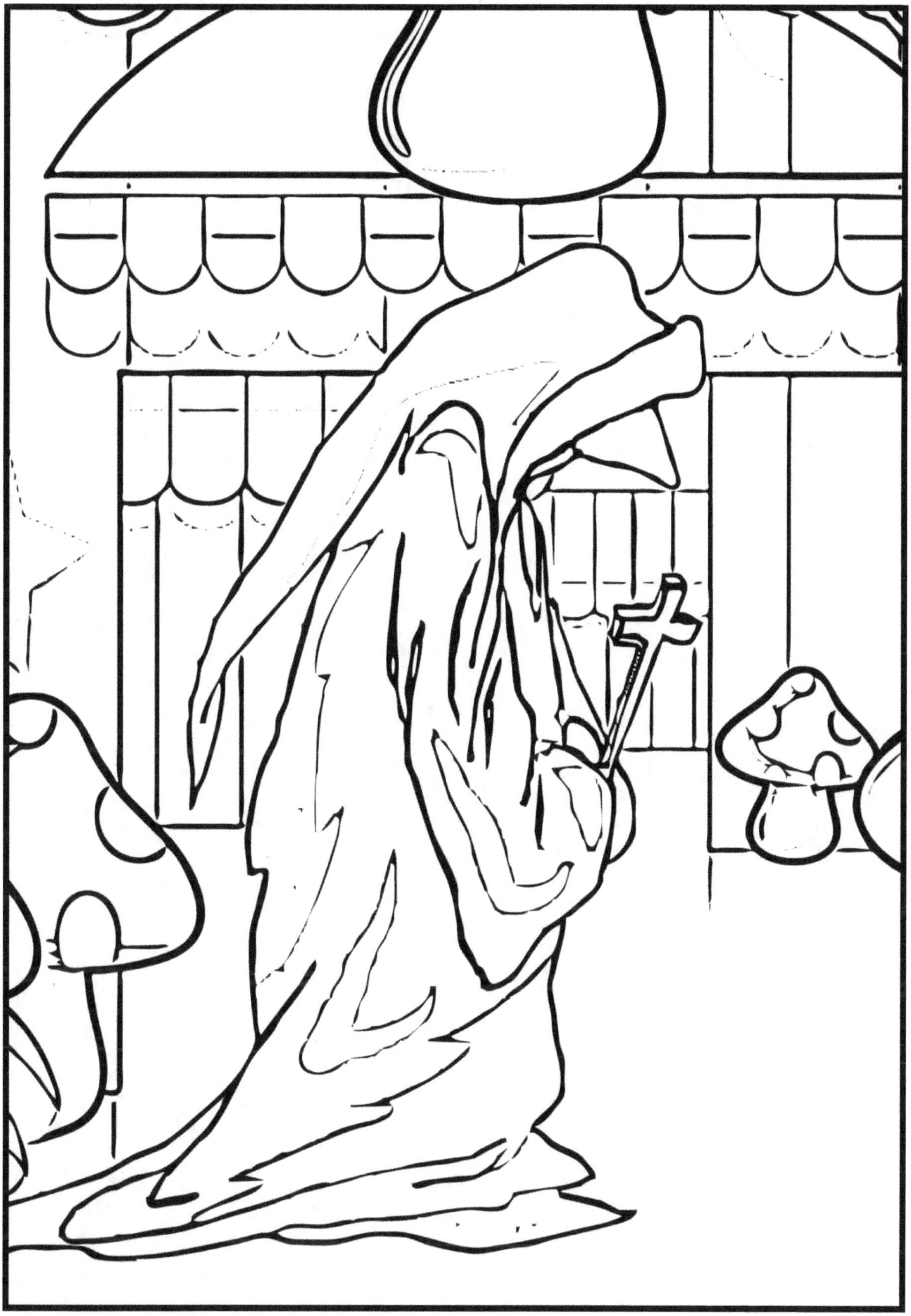

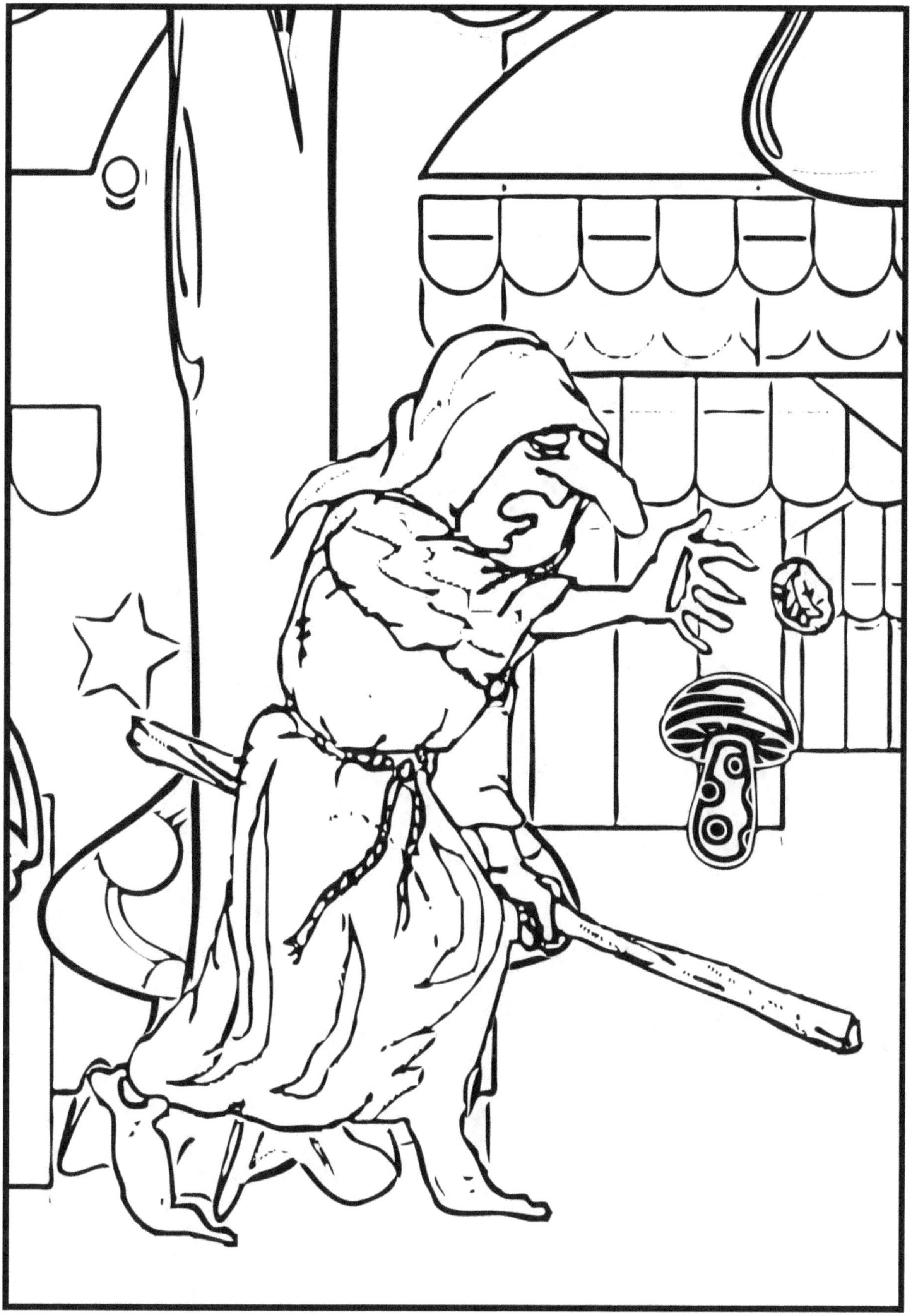

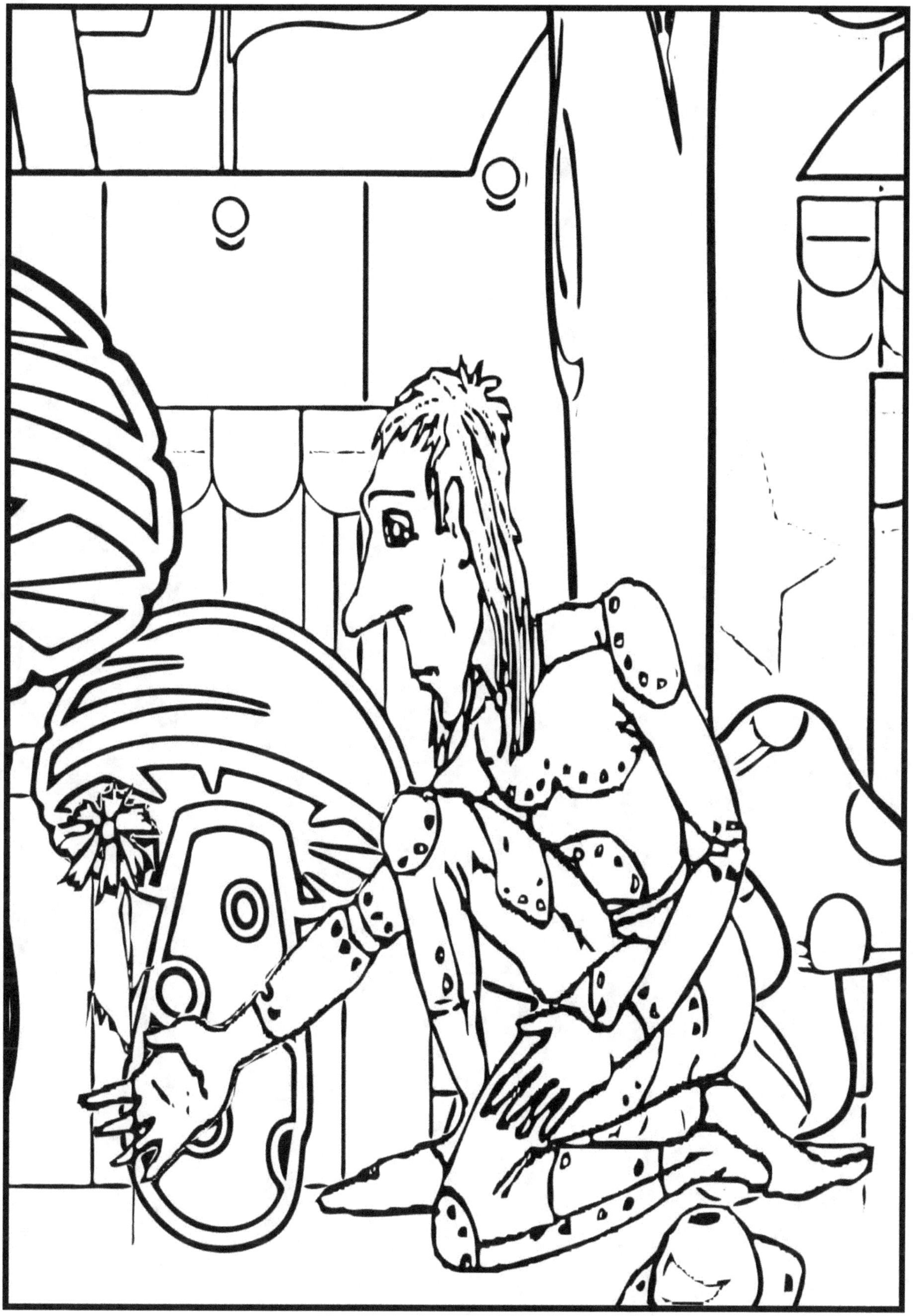

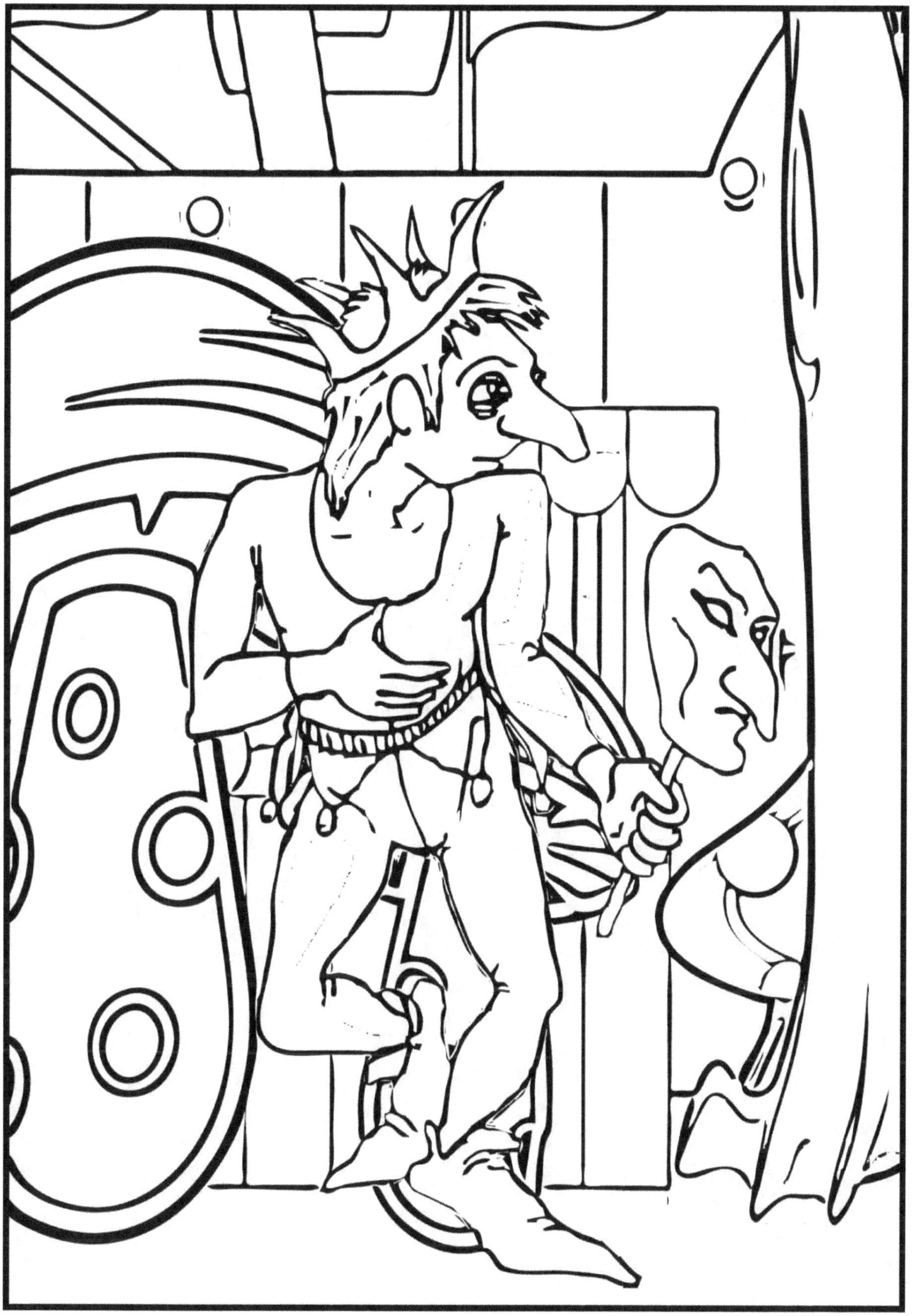

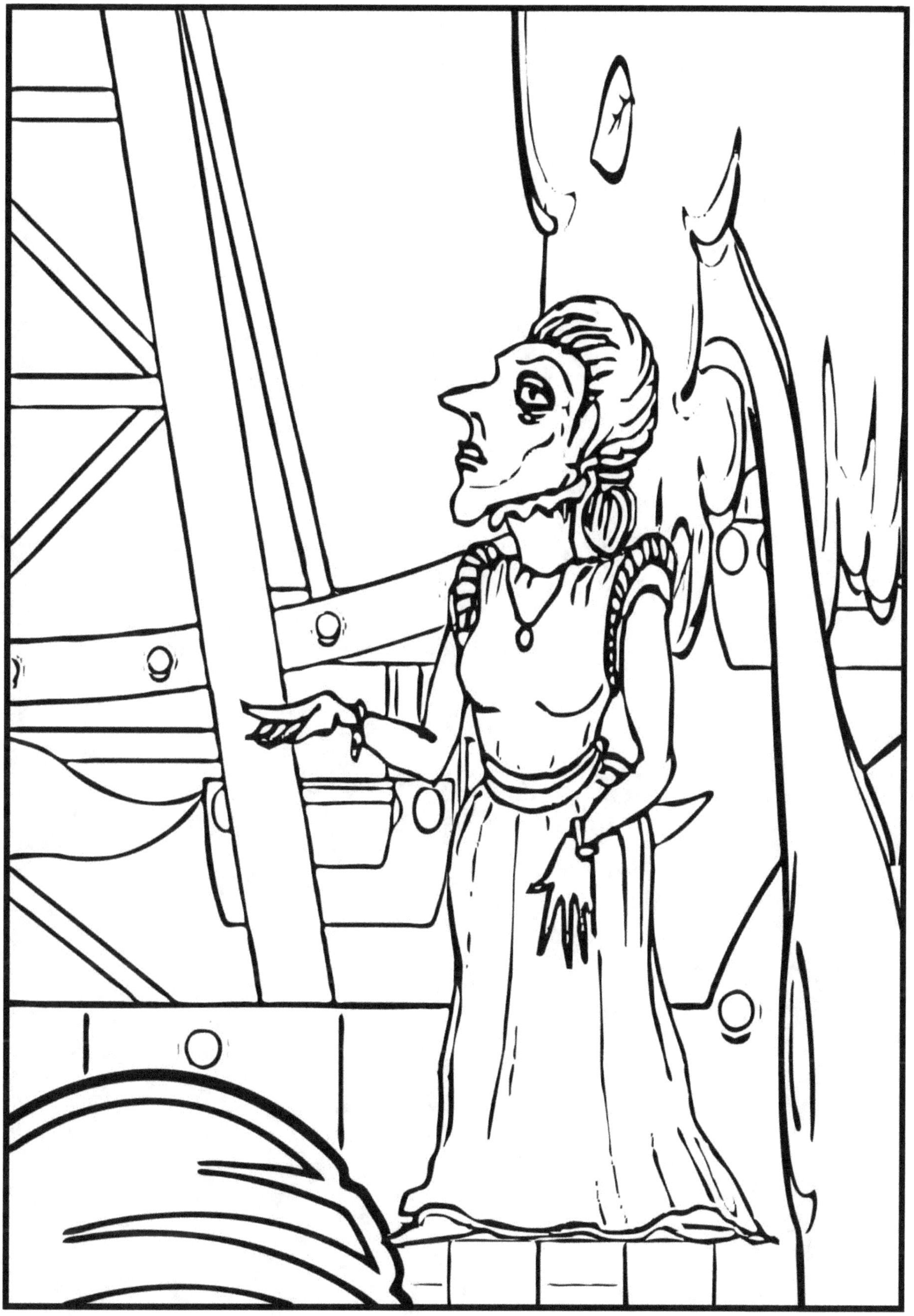

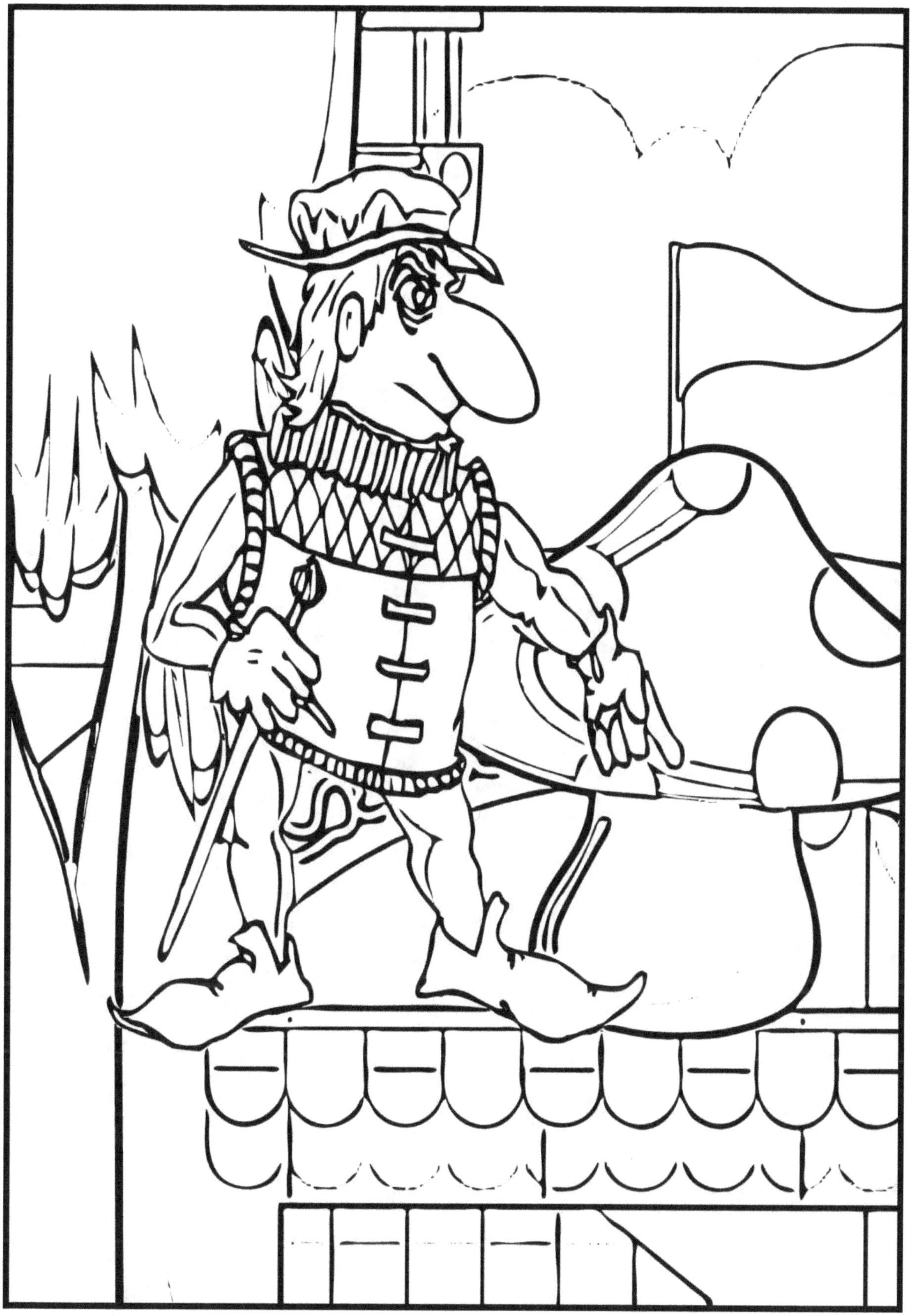

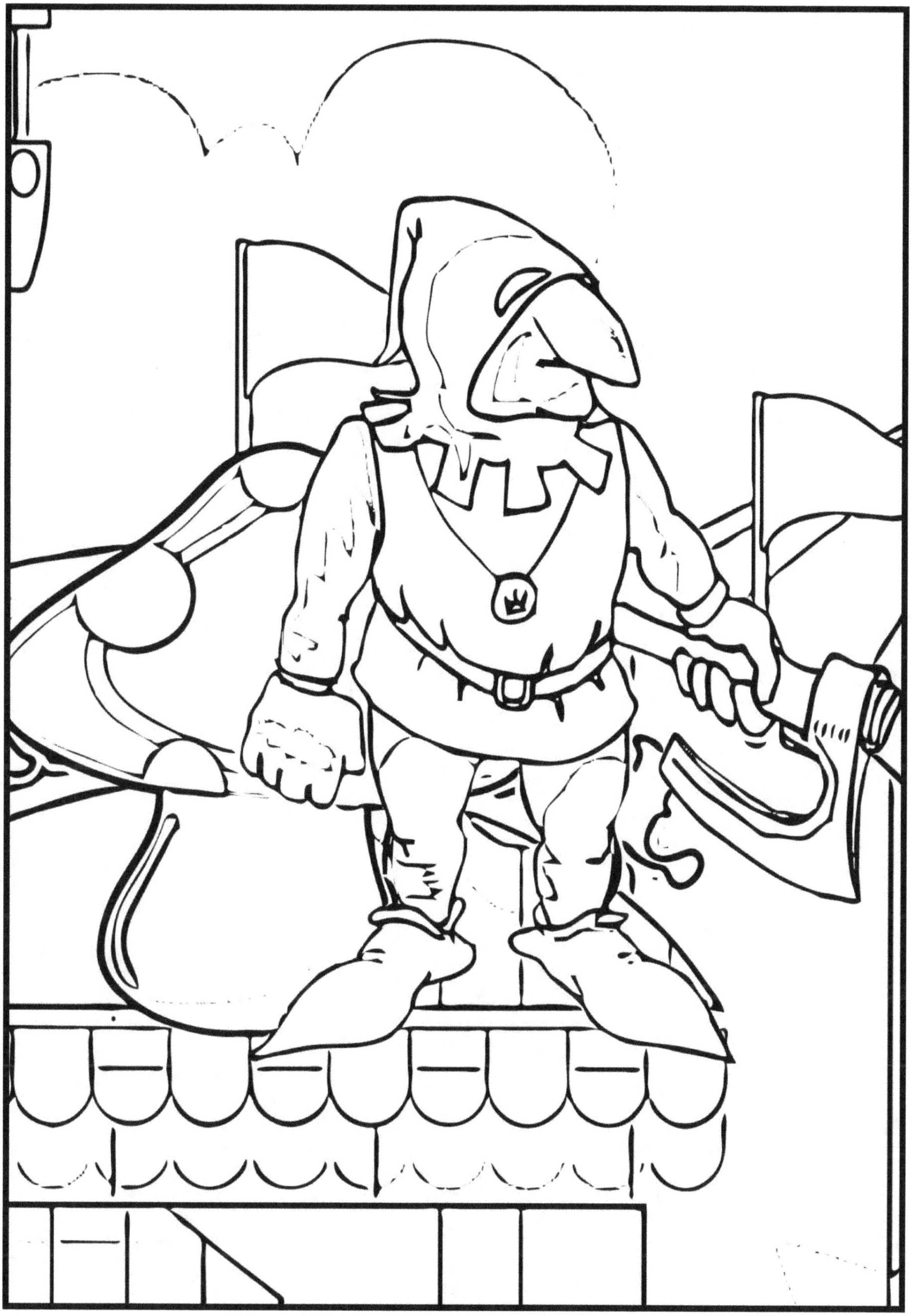

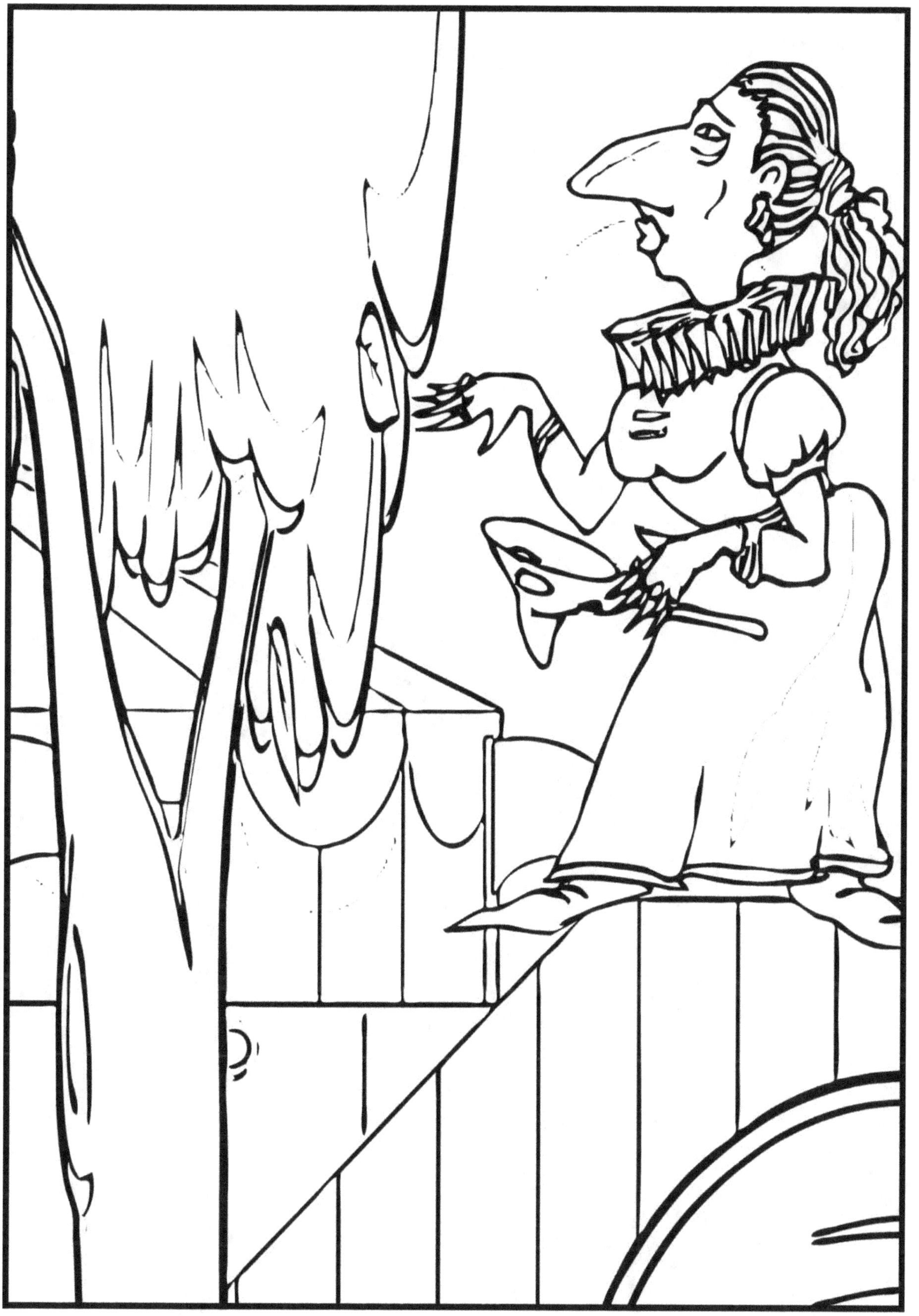

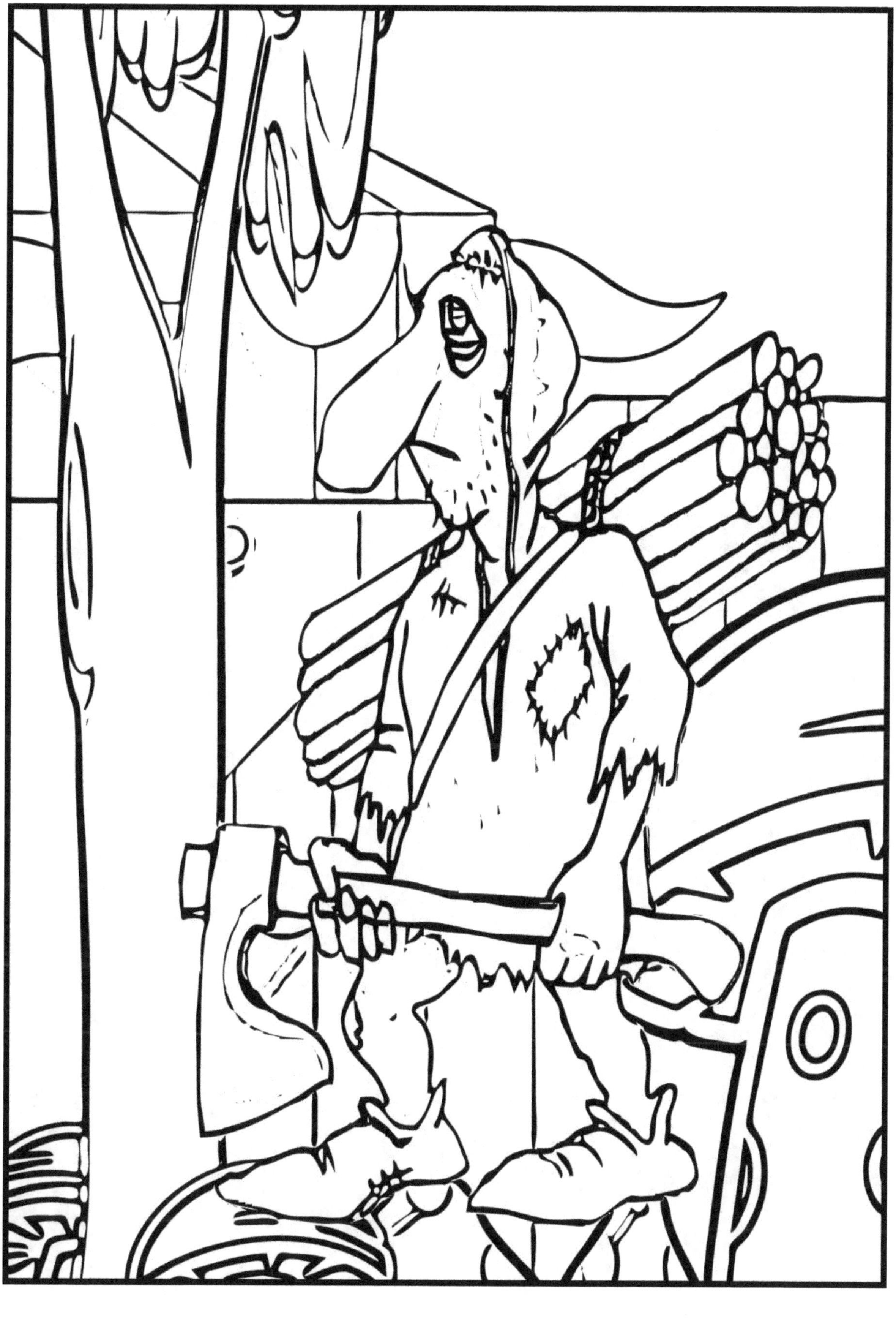

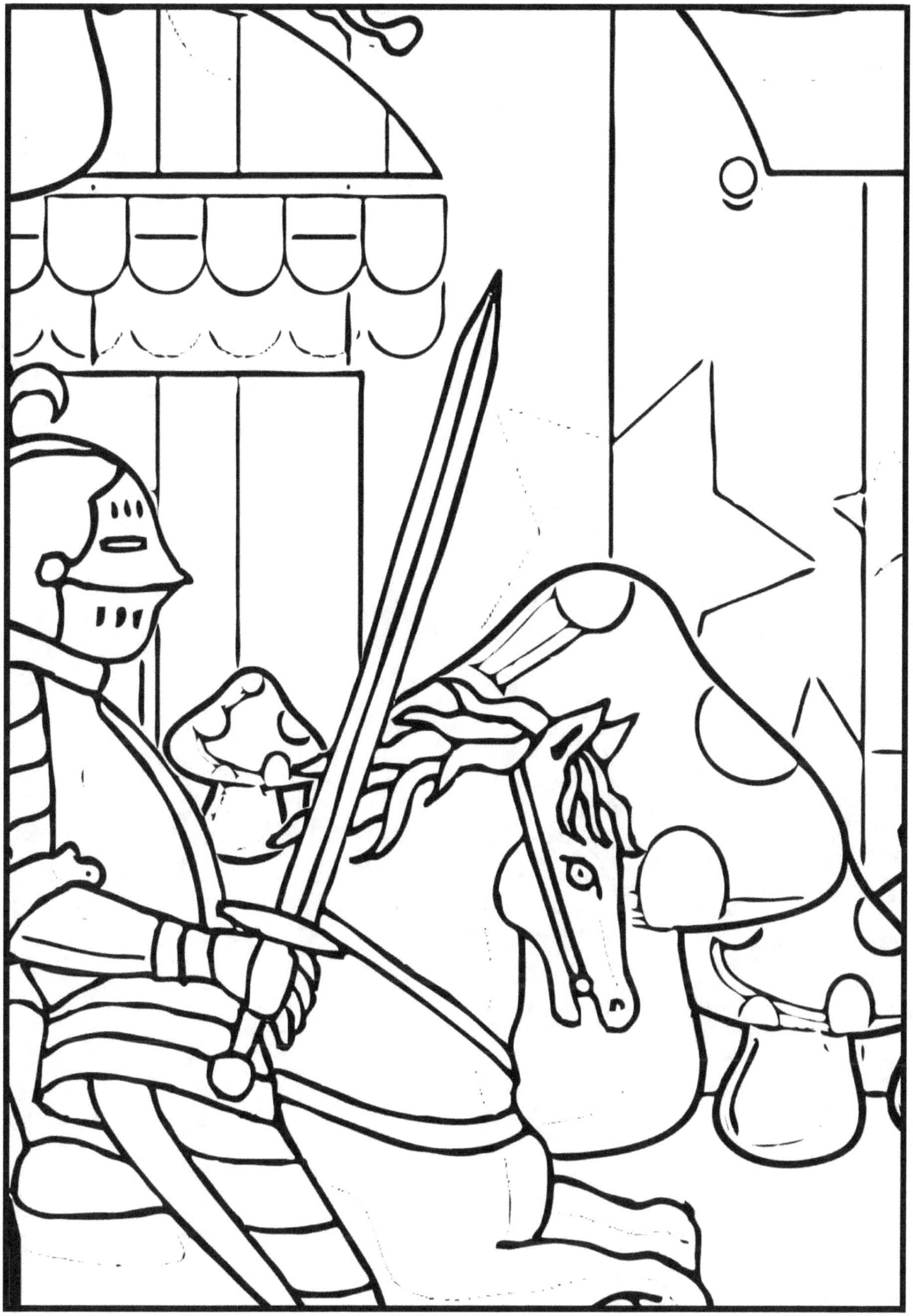

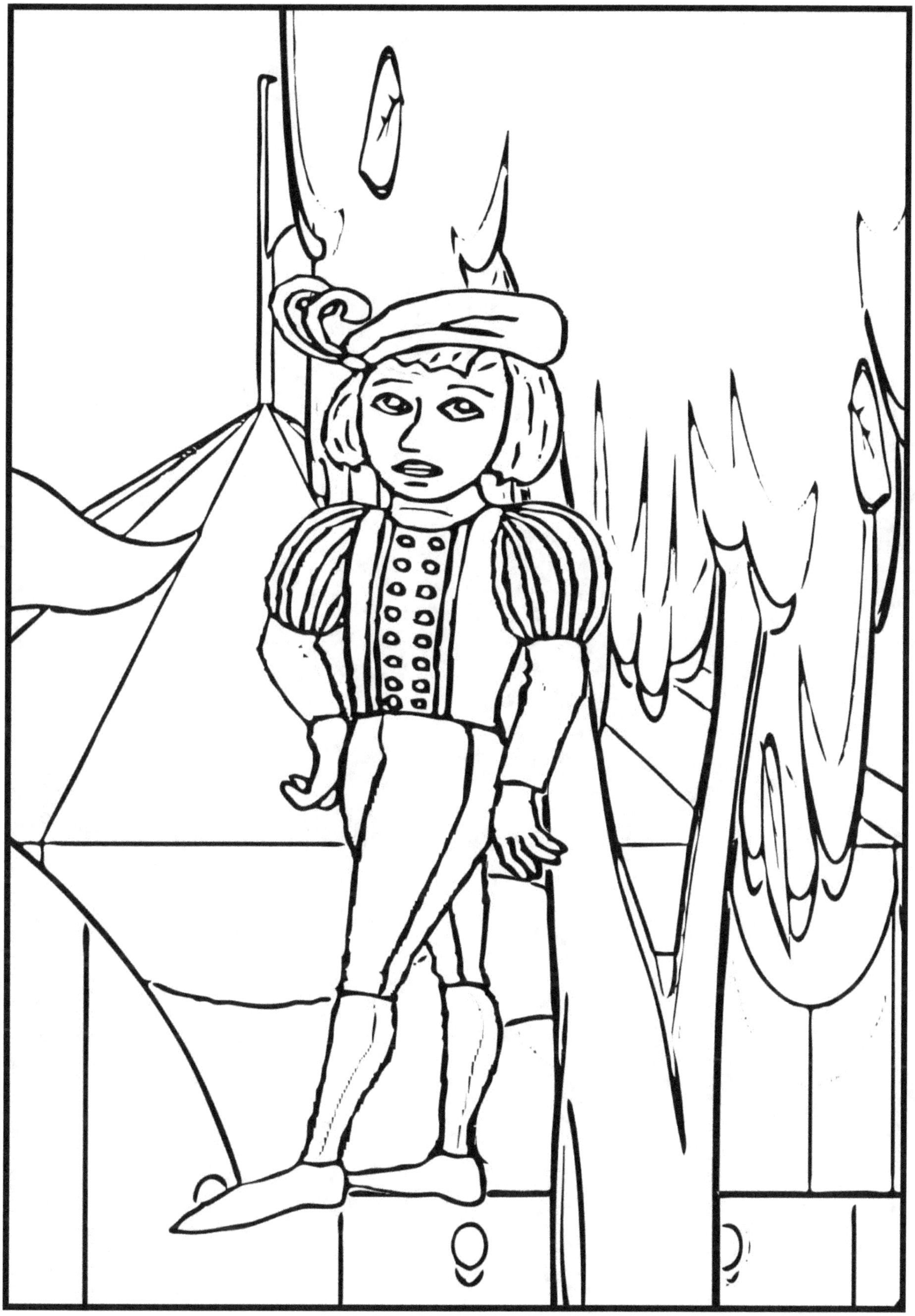

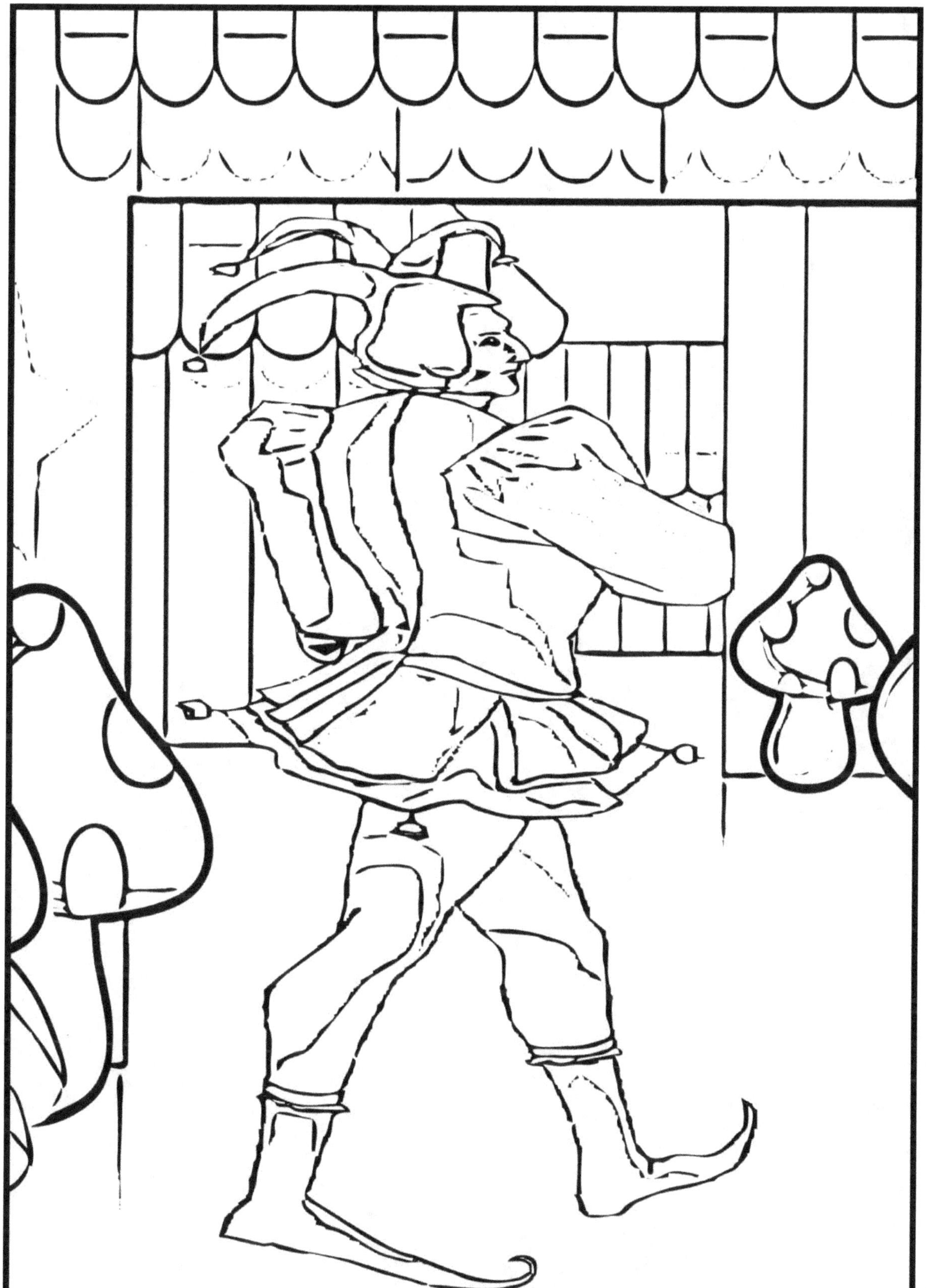

Remarkable ROMANS Coloring Book

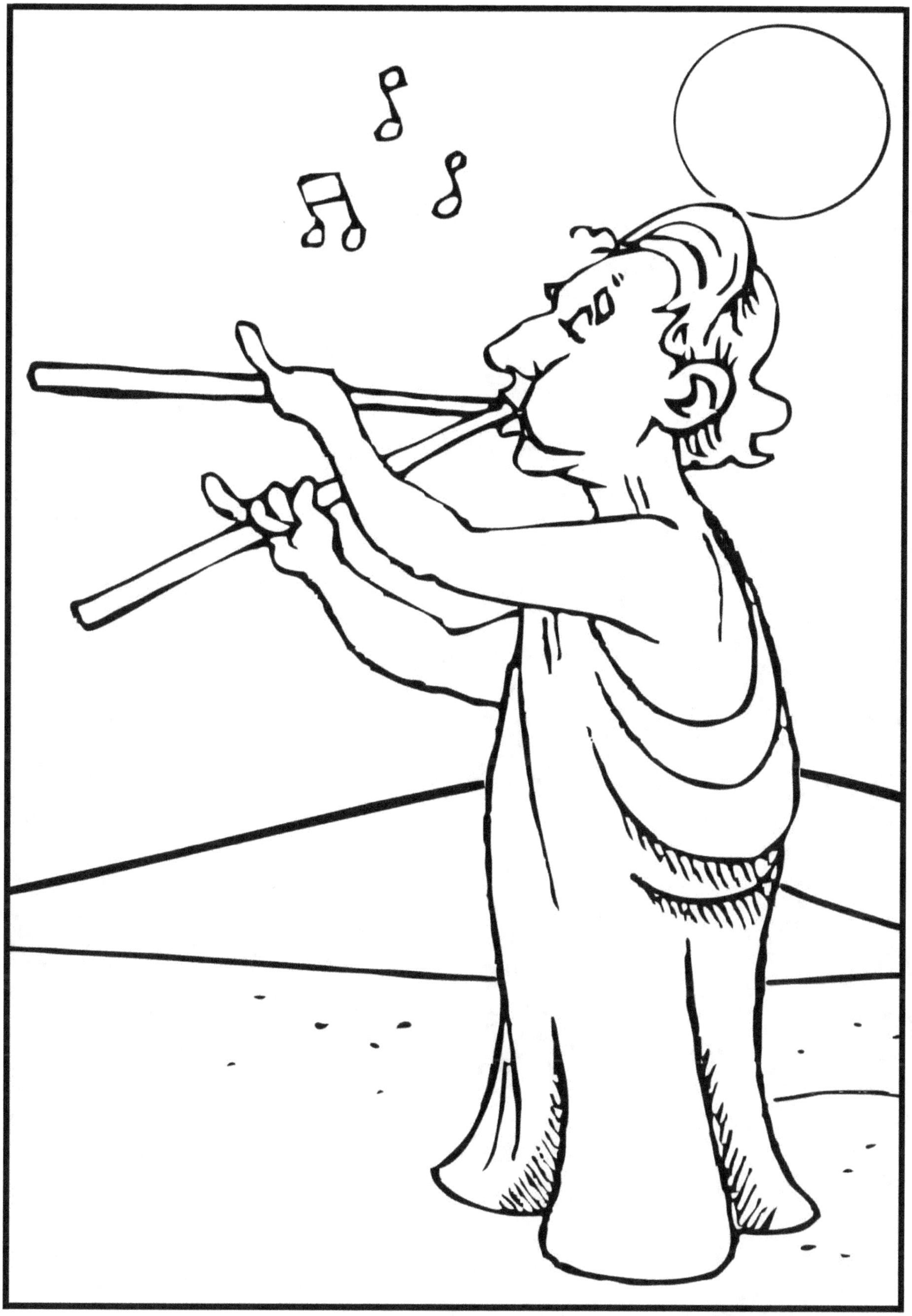

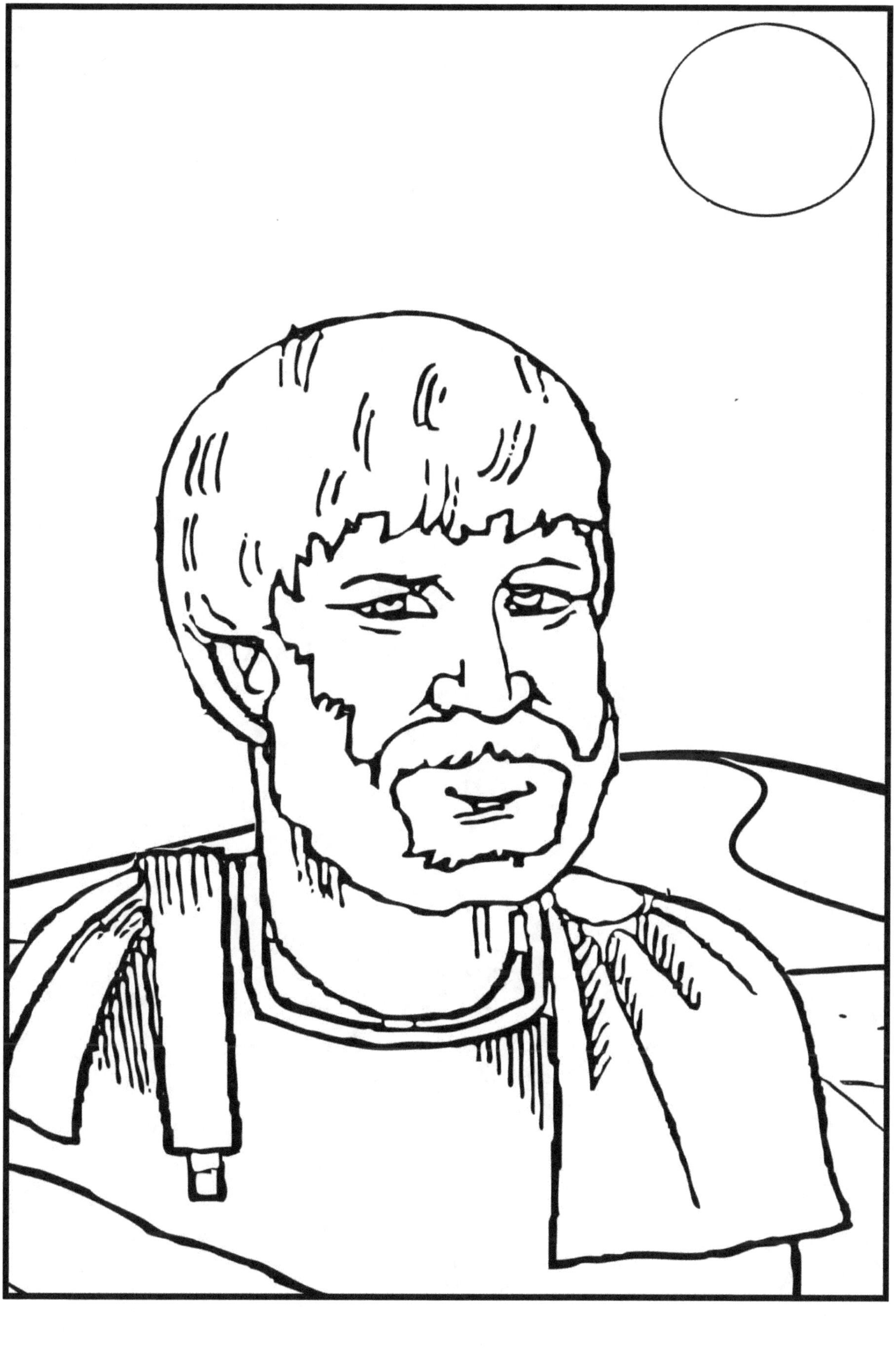

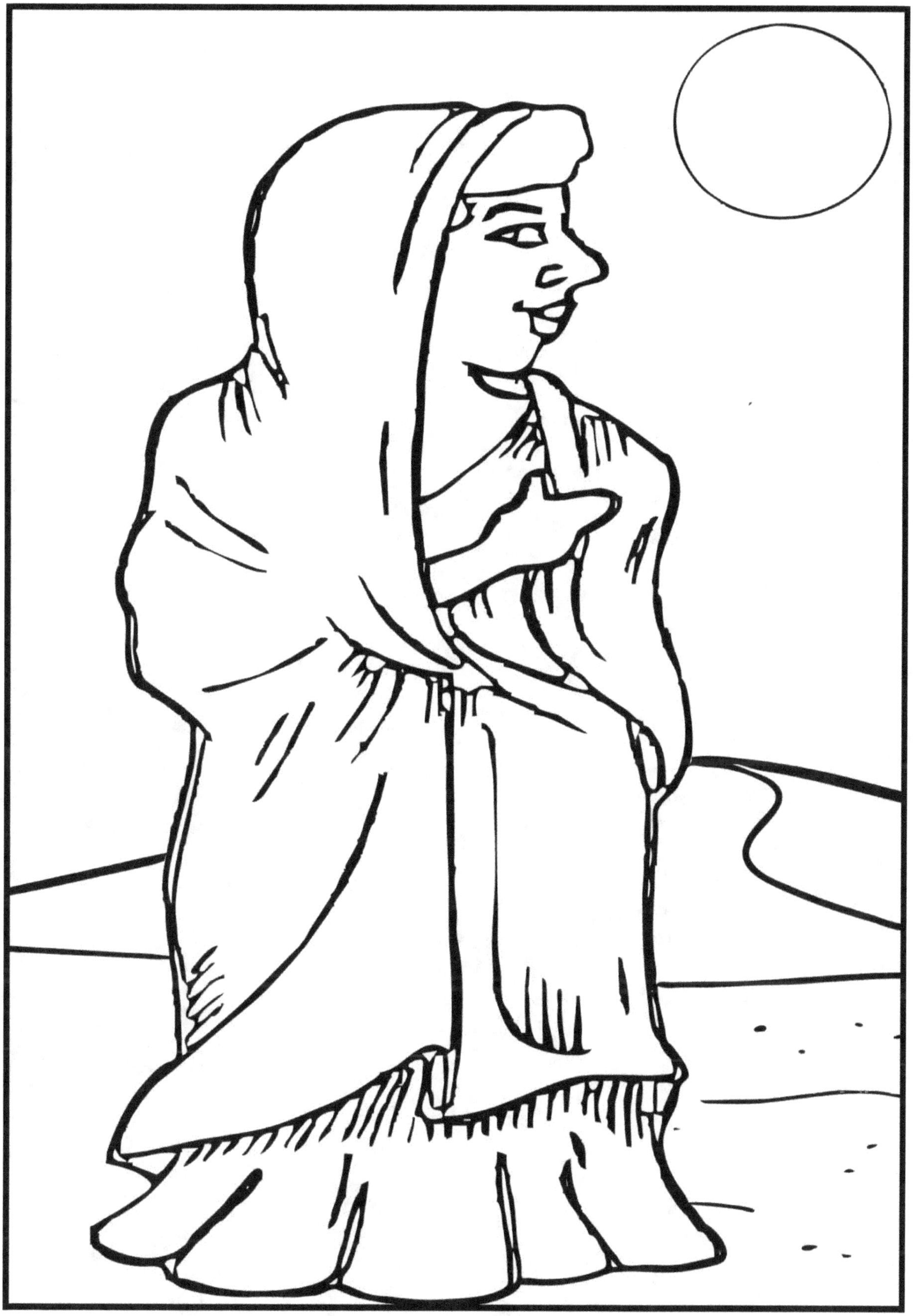

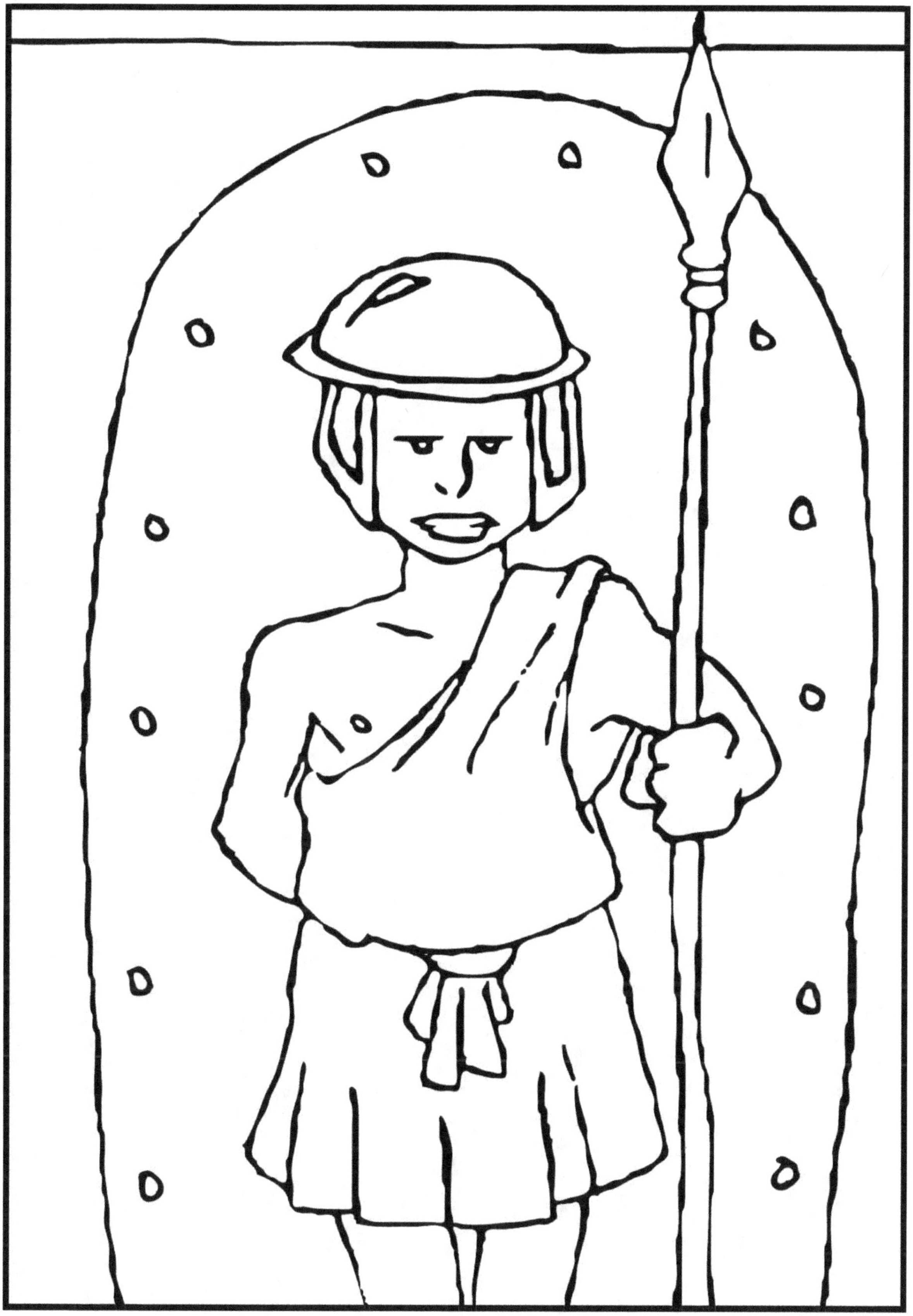

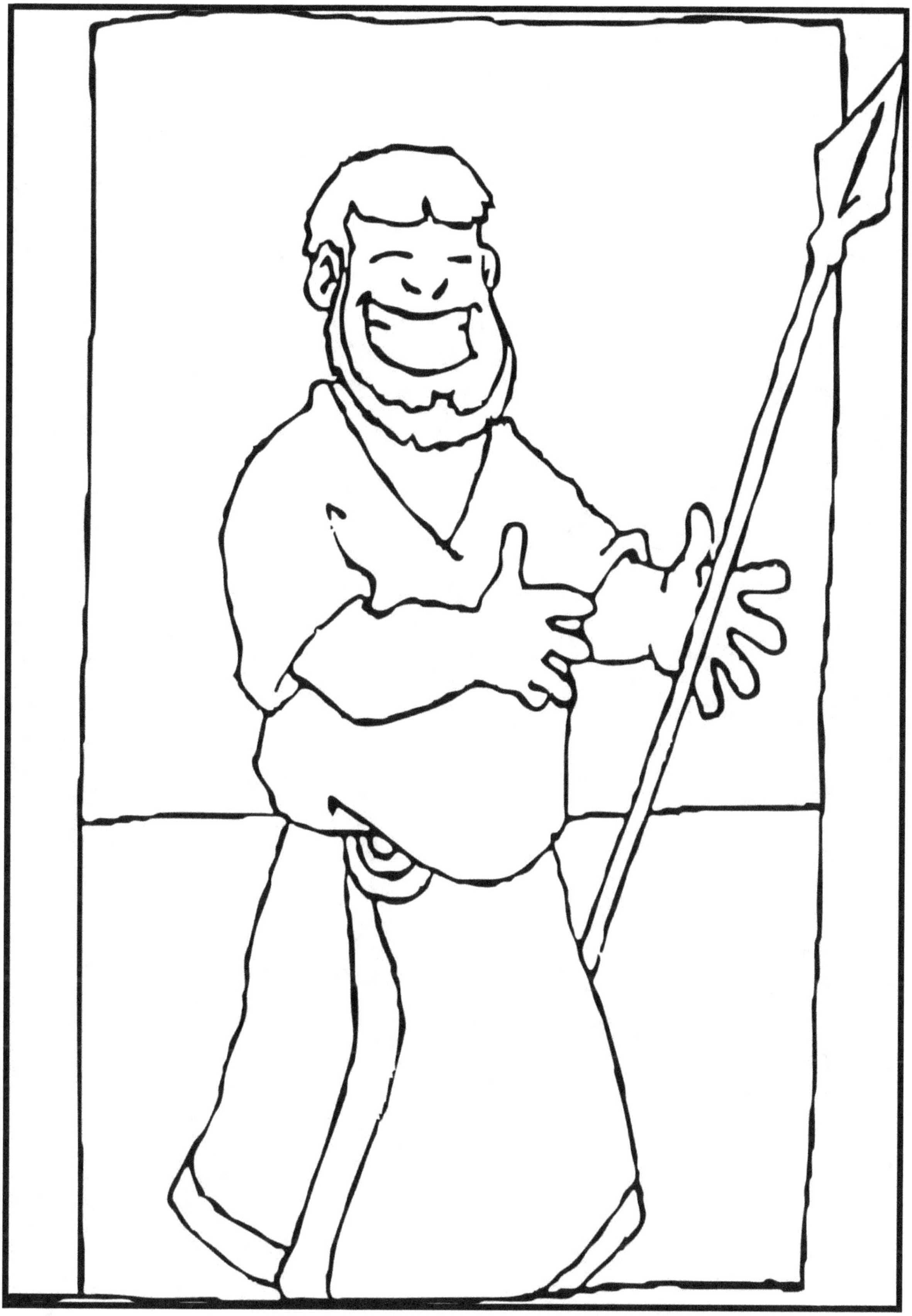

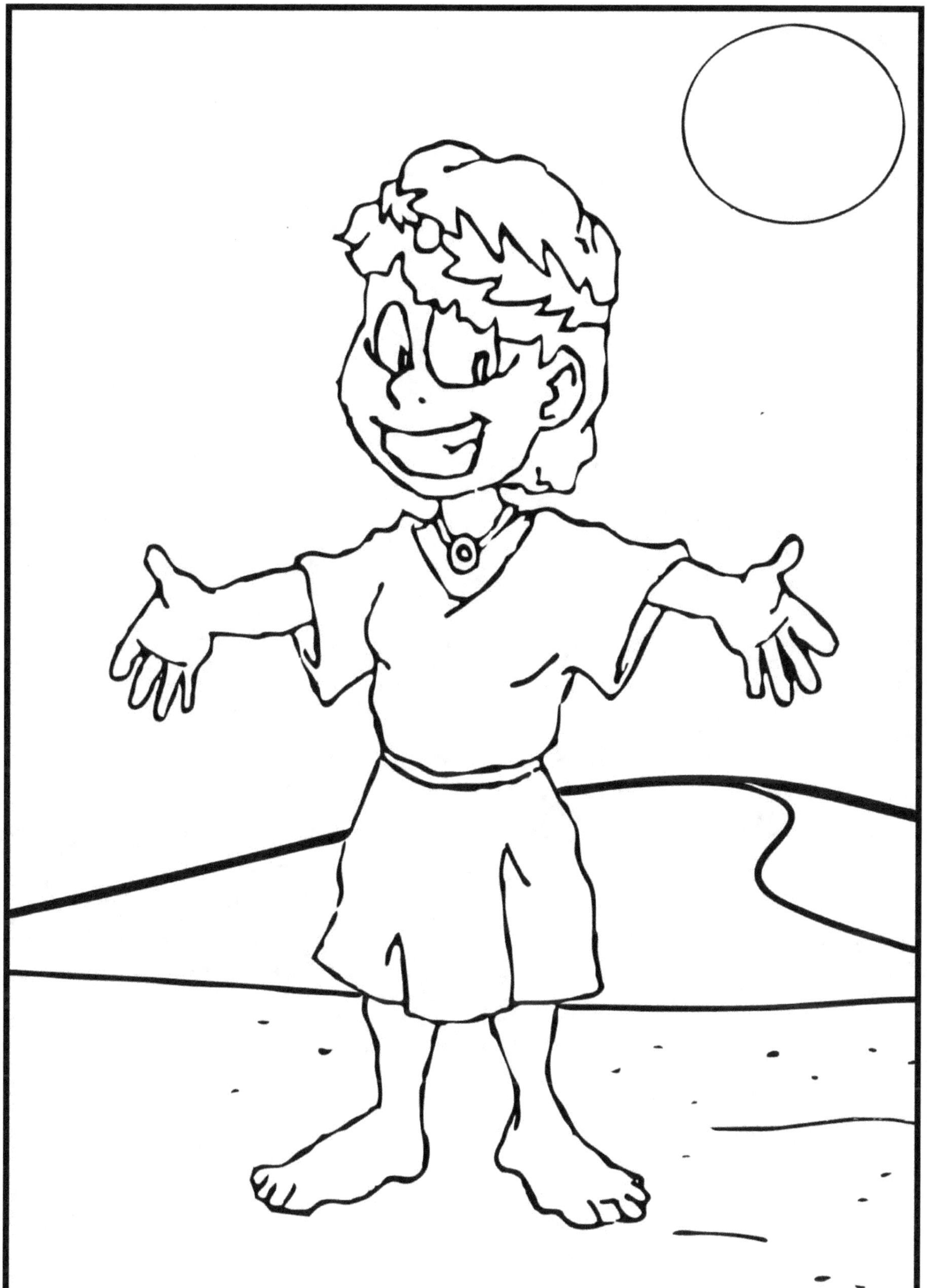

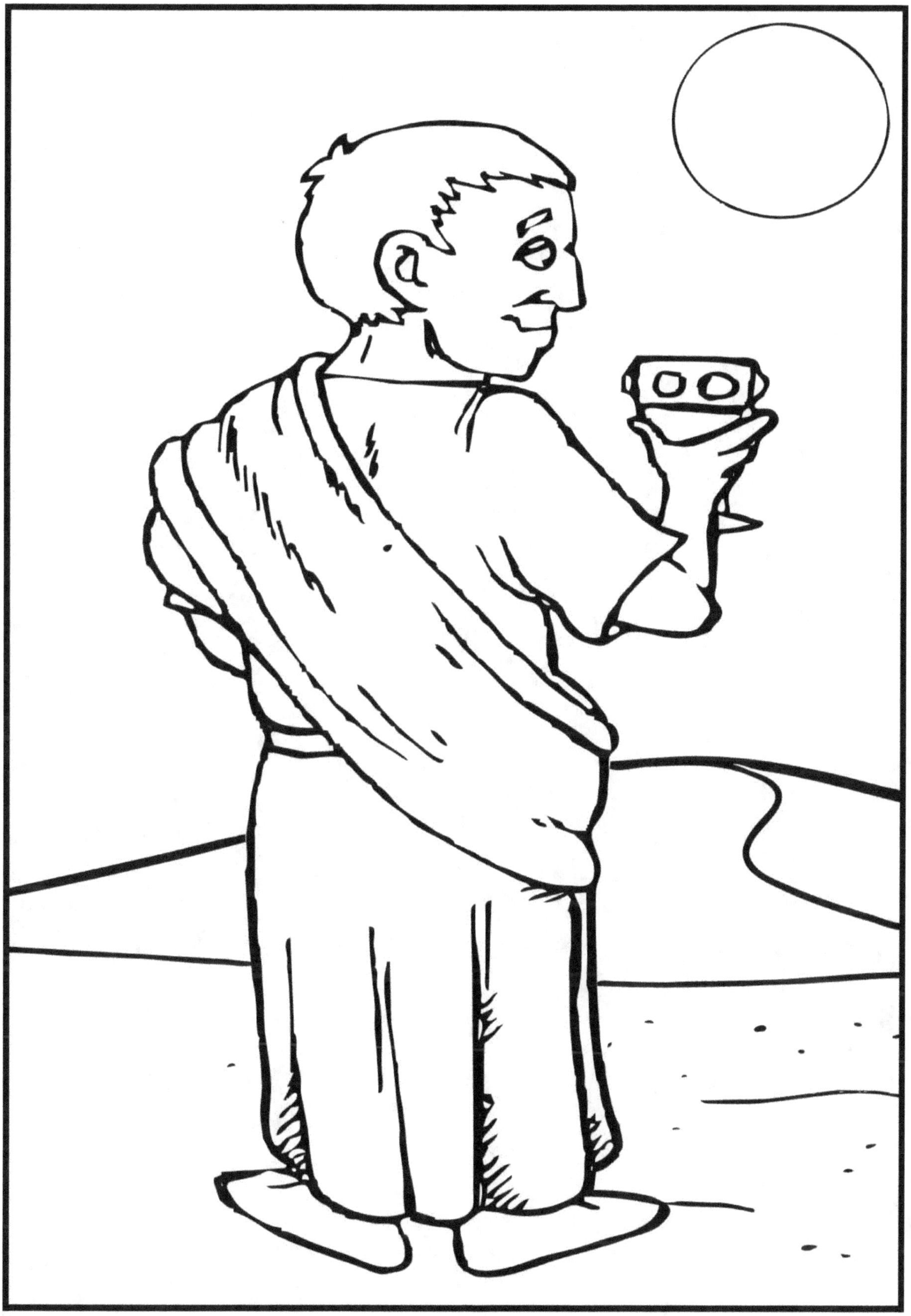

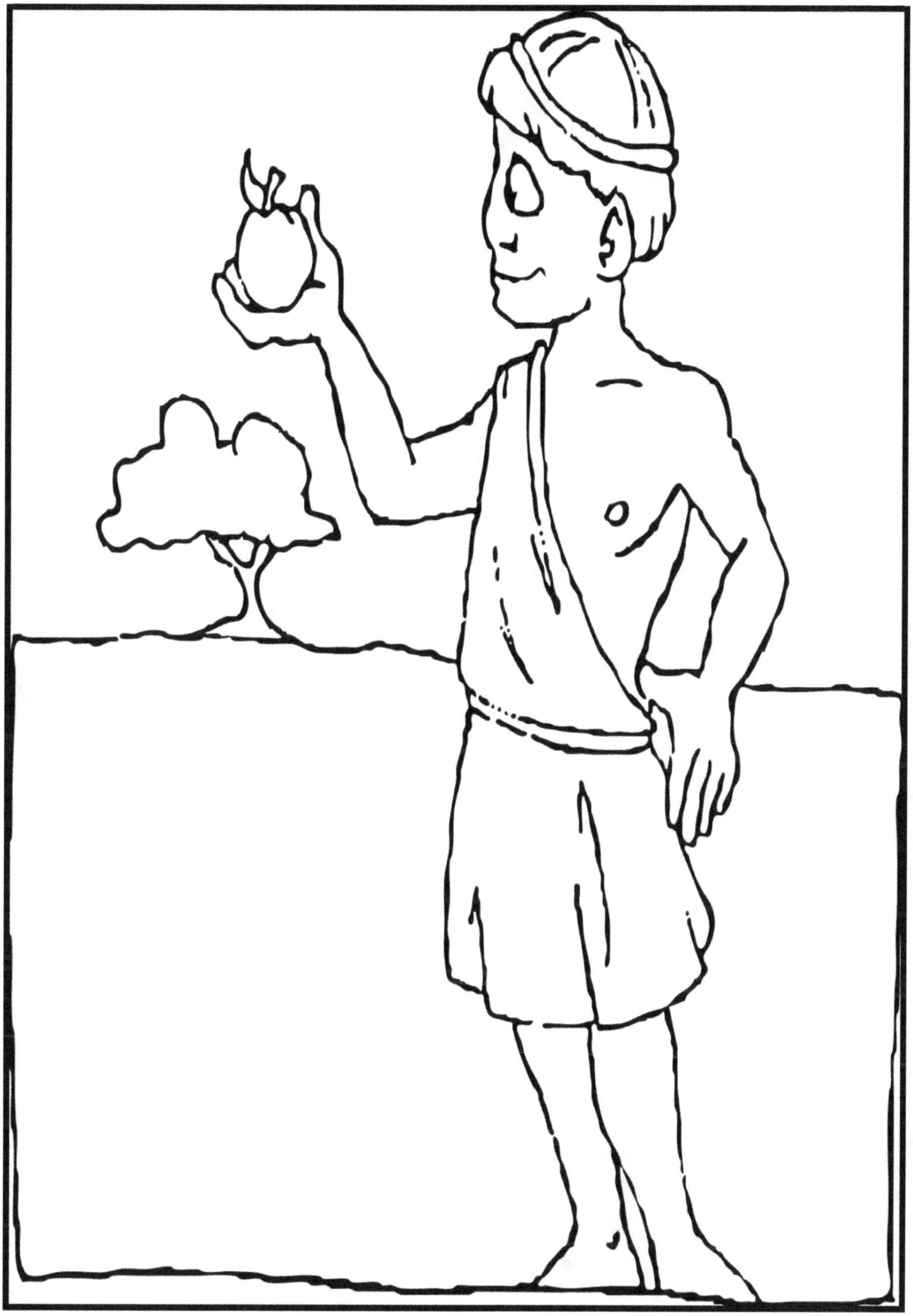

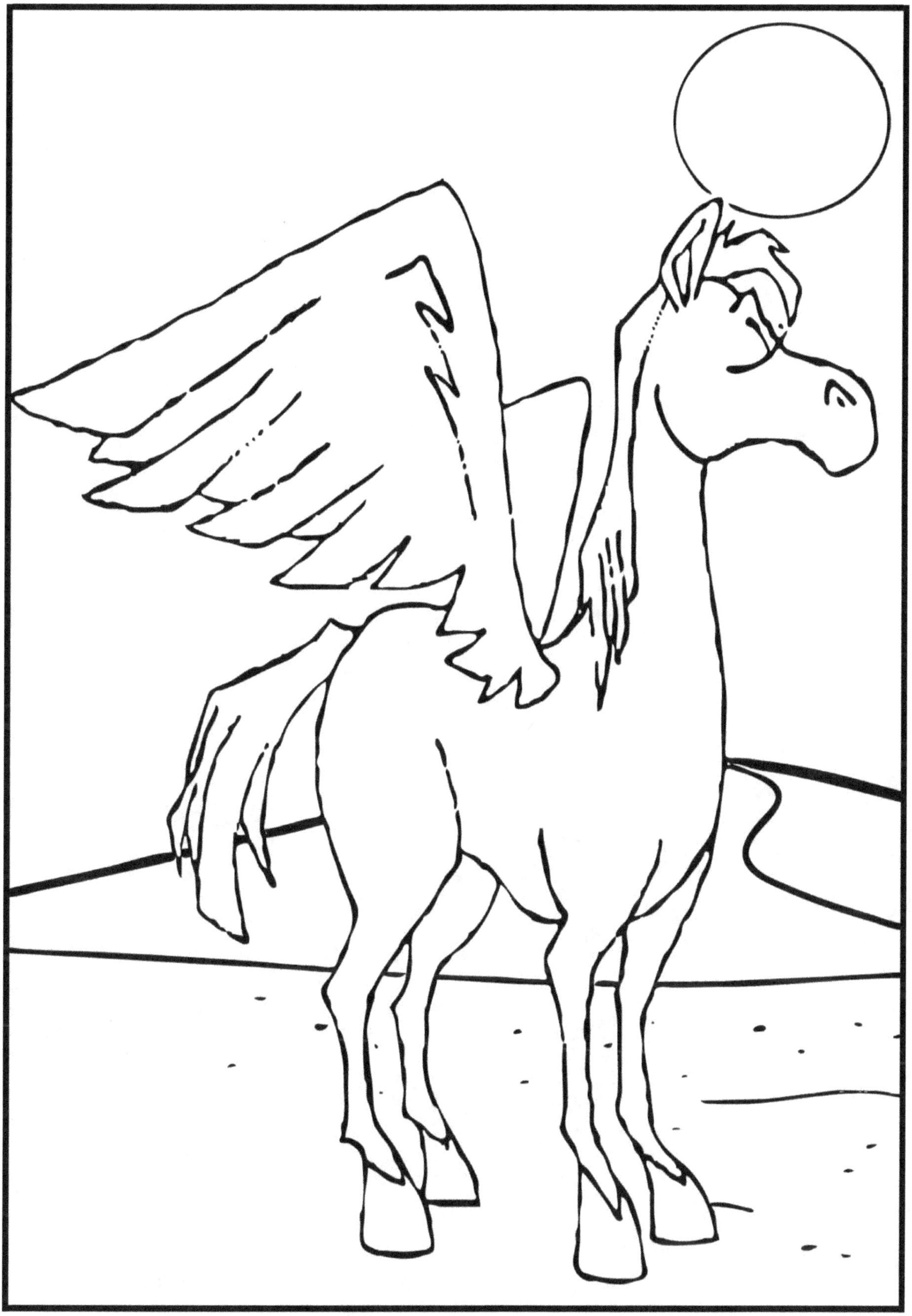

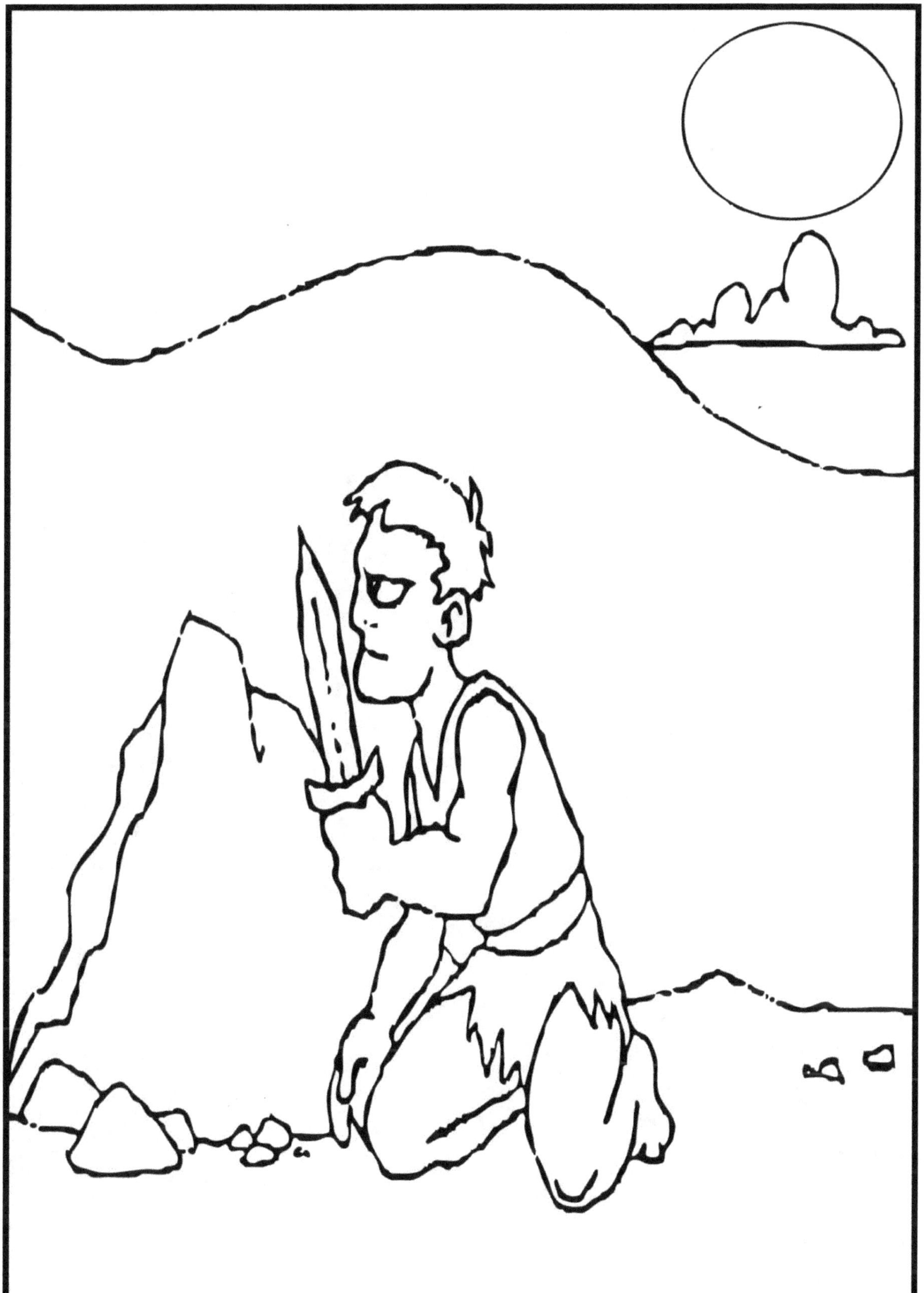

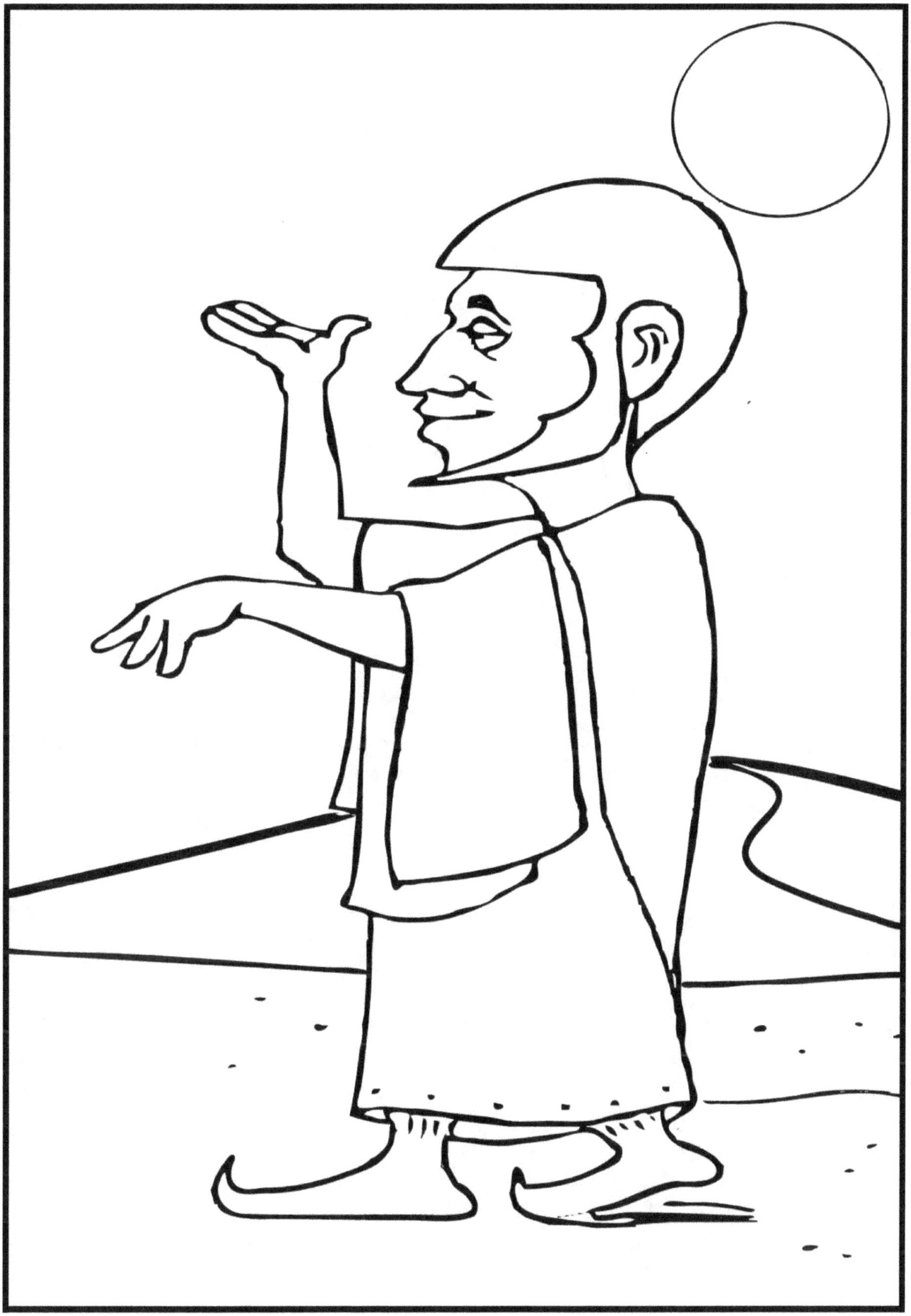

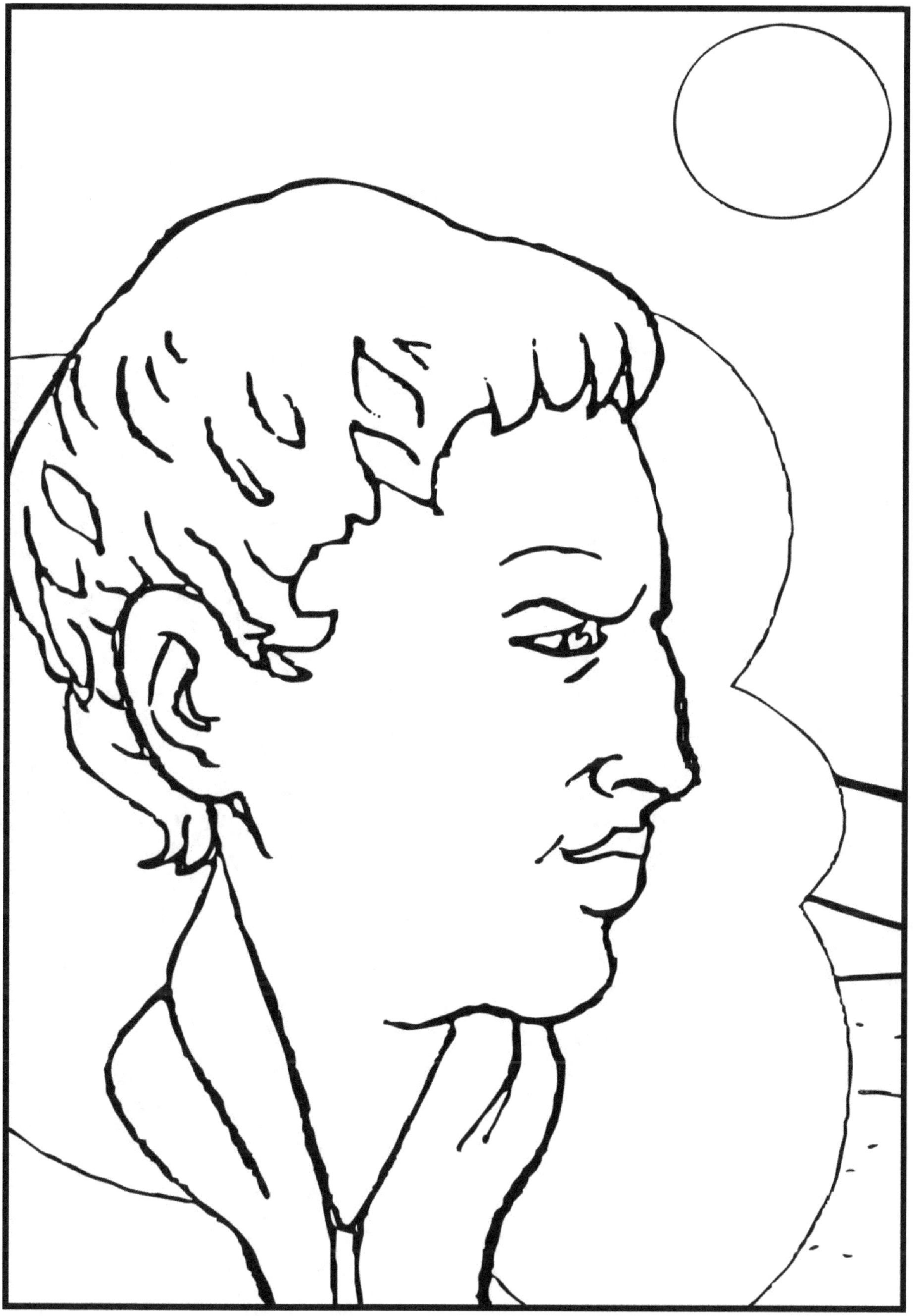

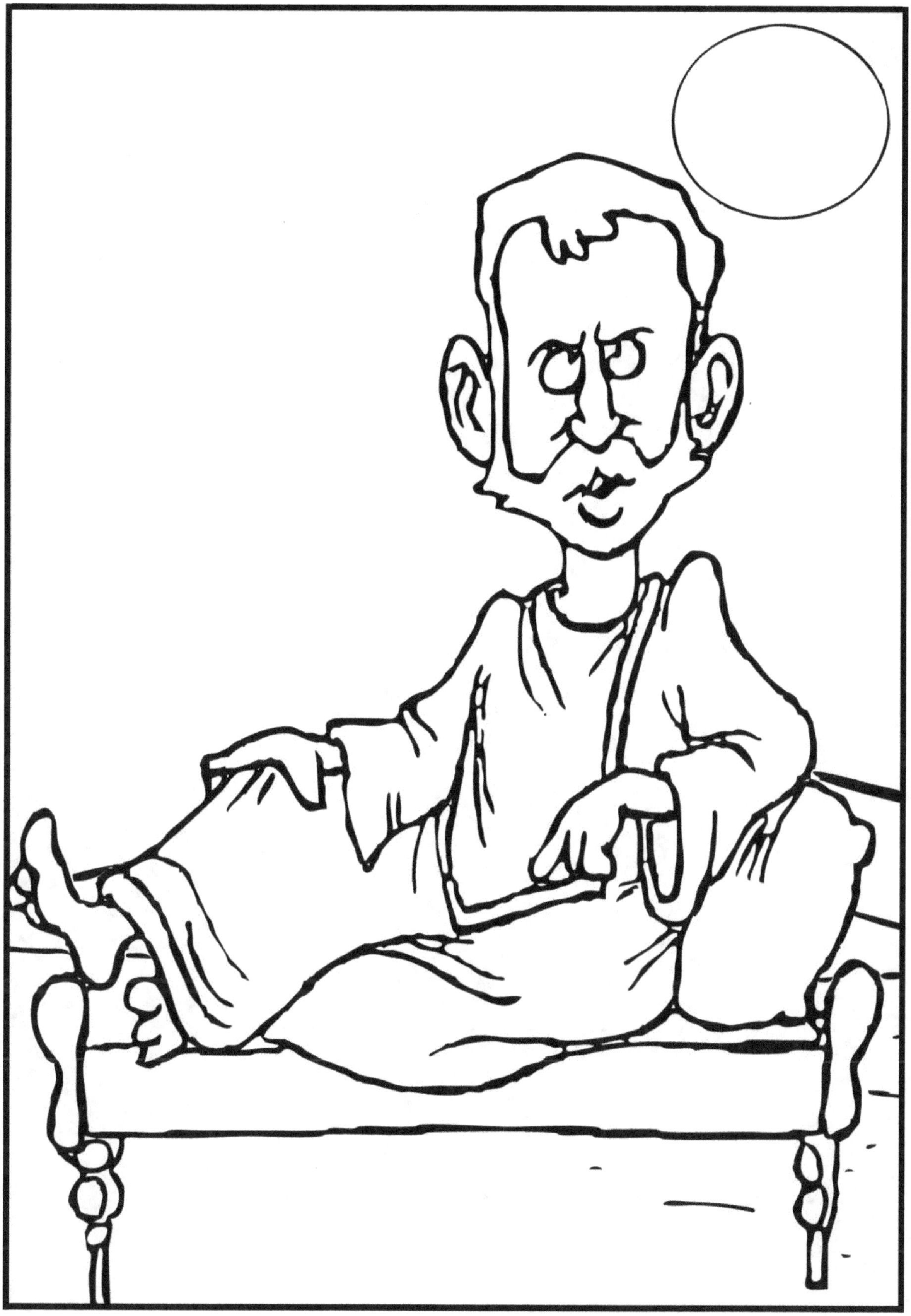

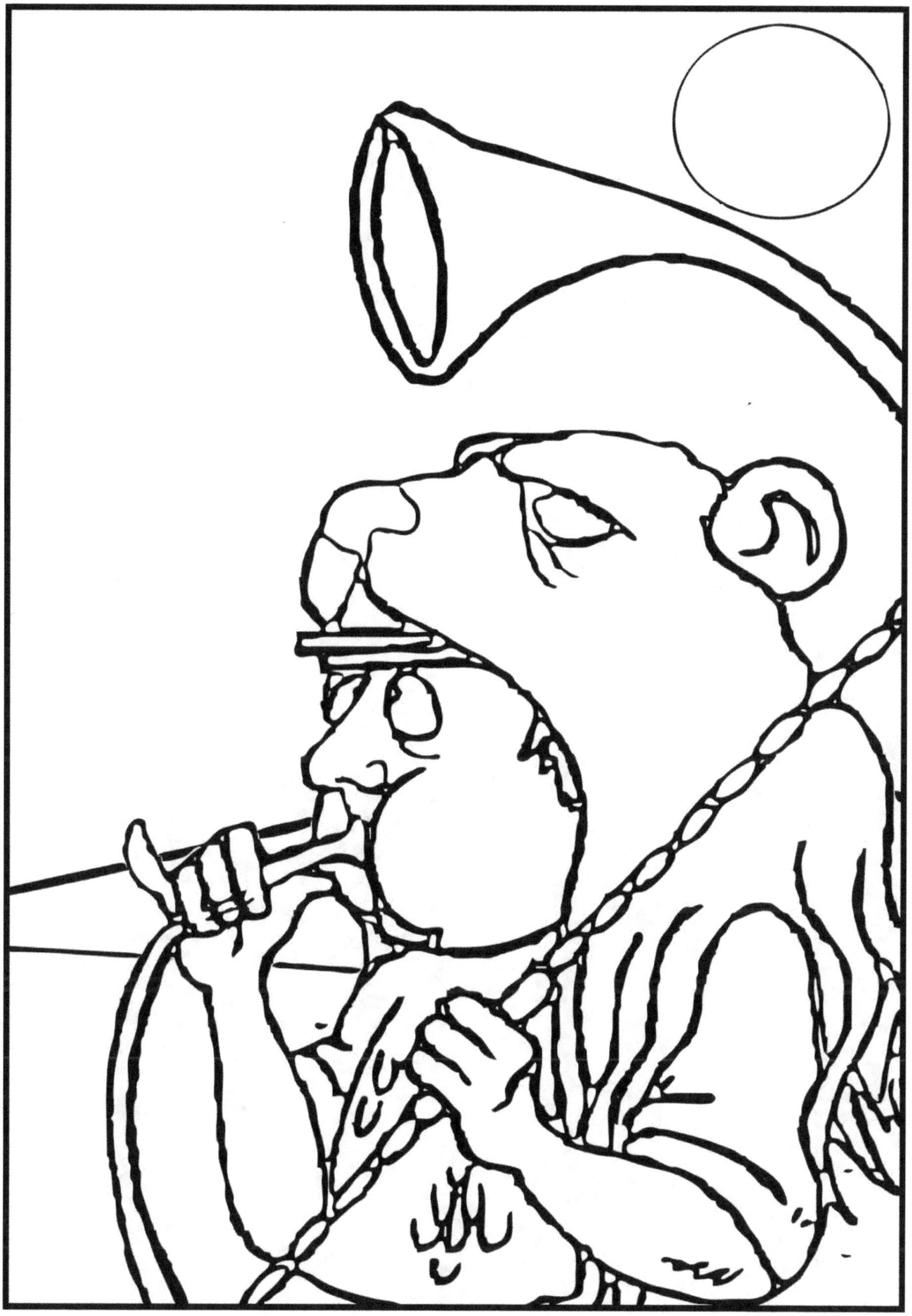

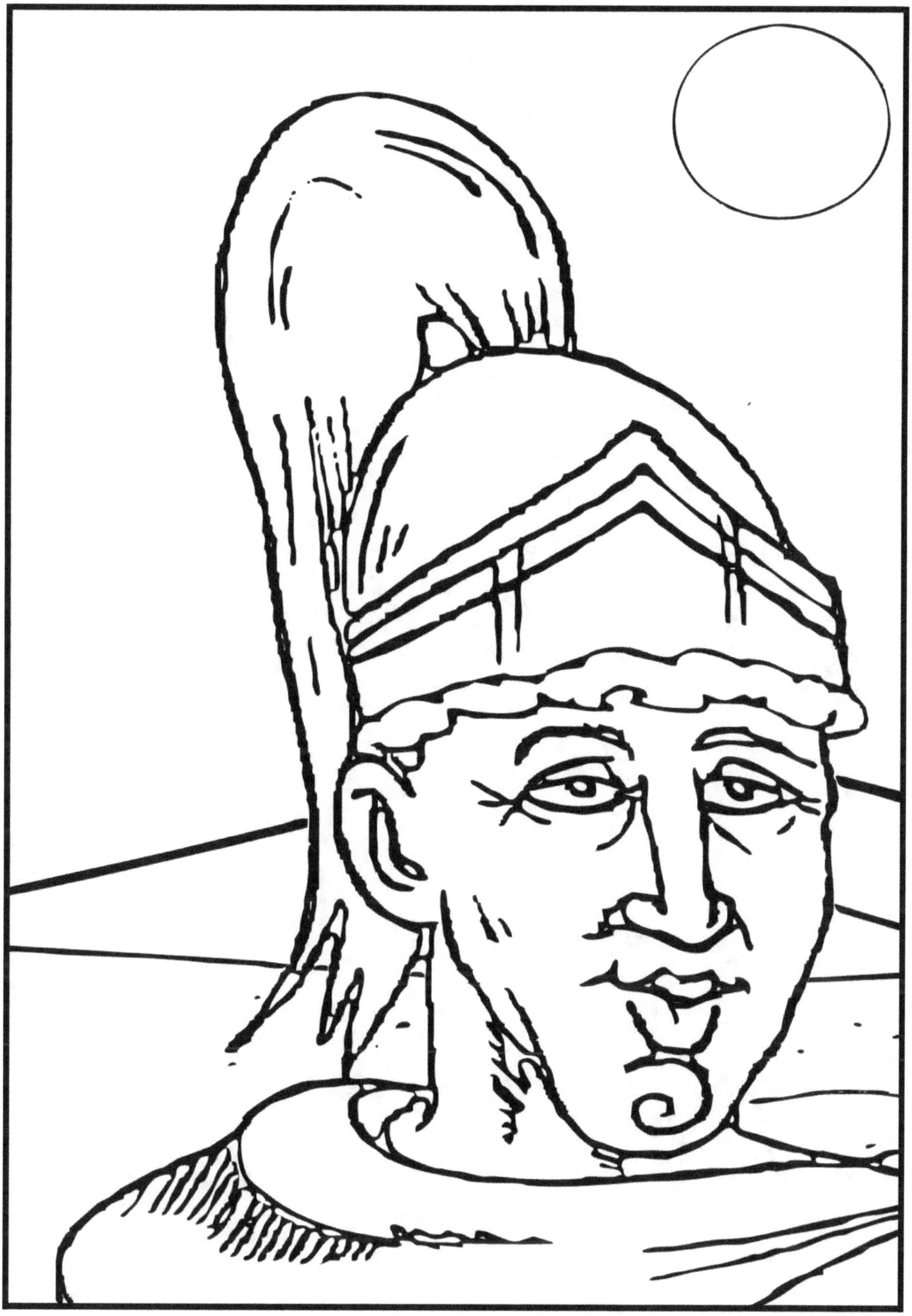

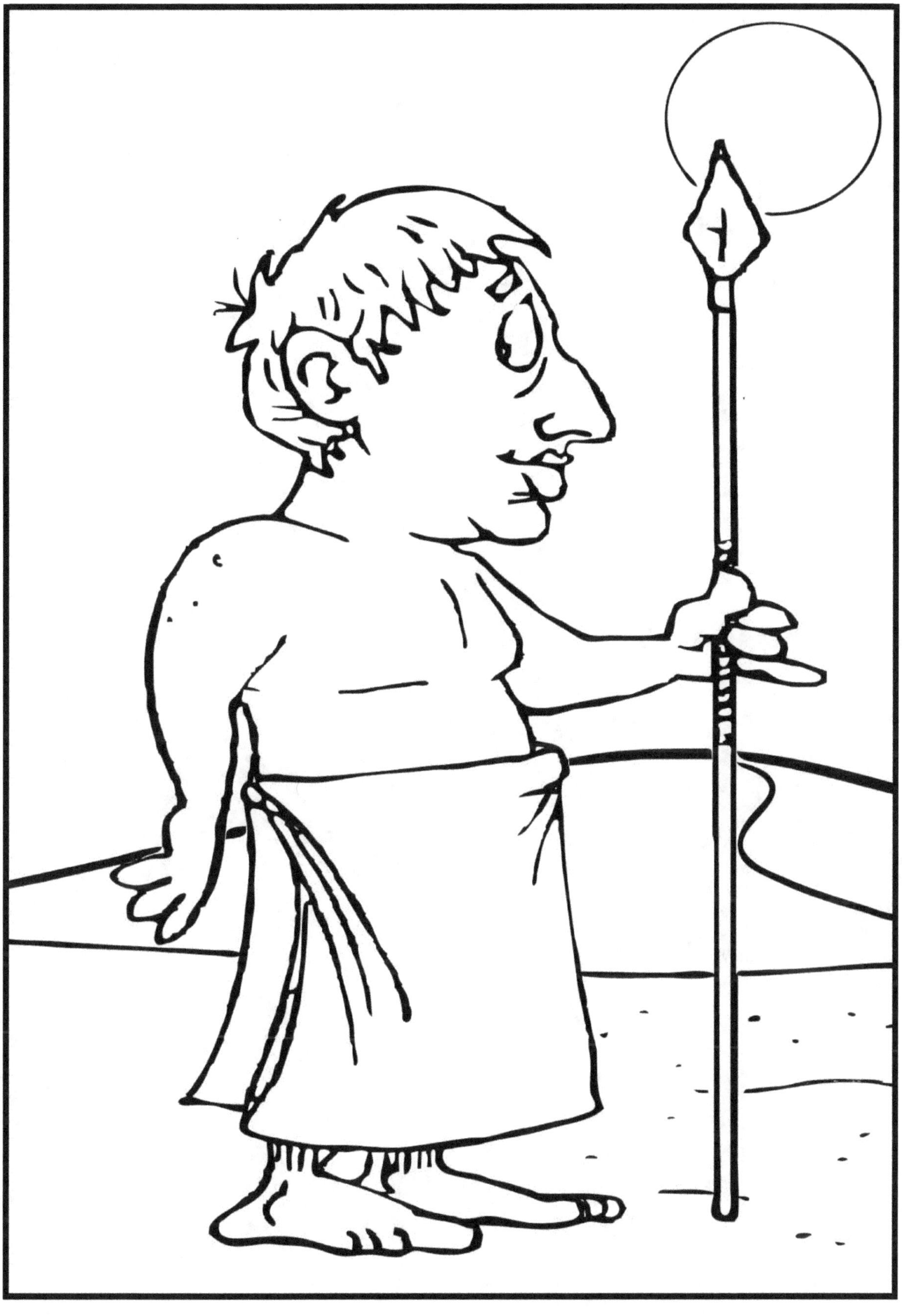

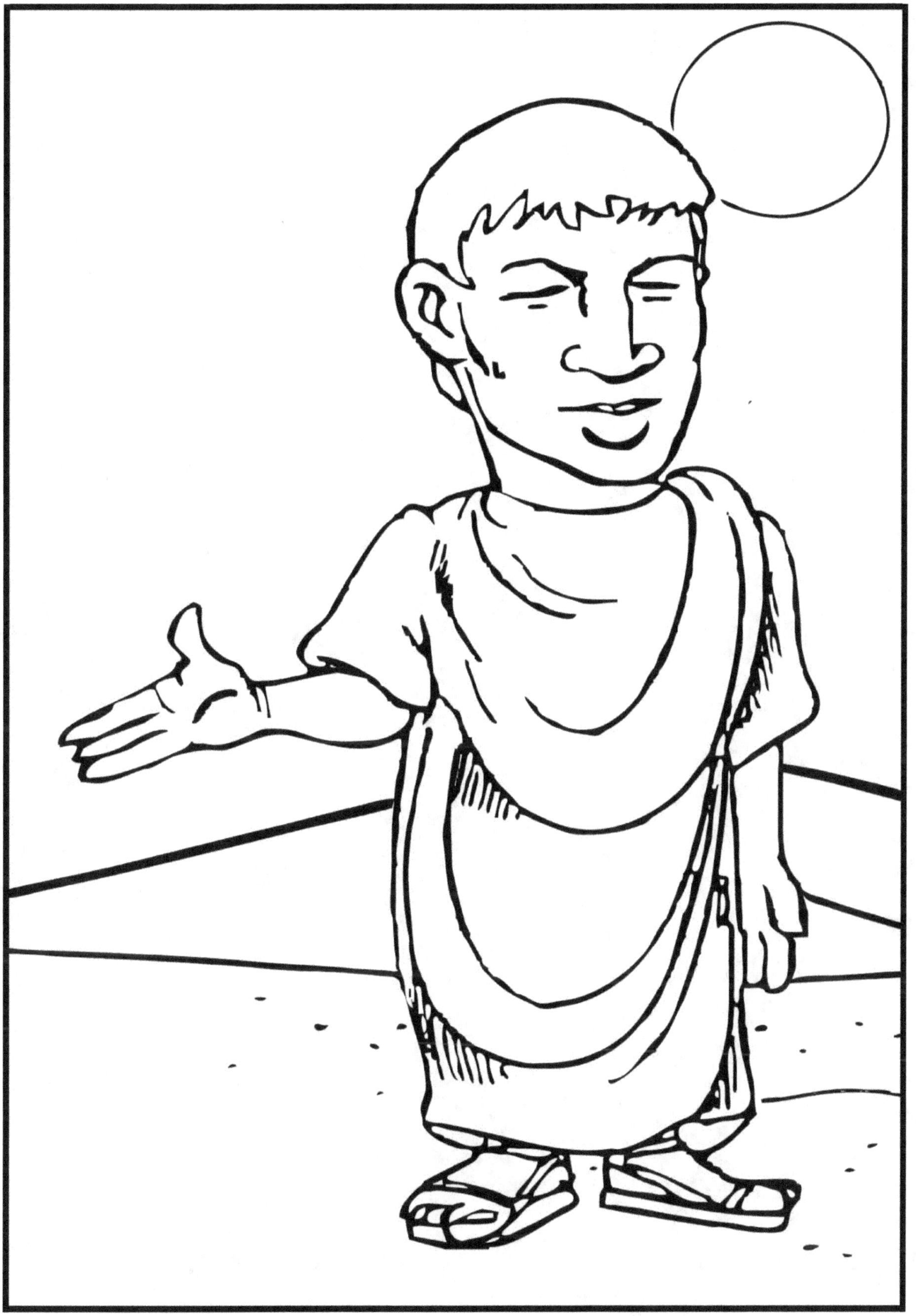

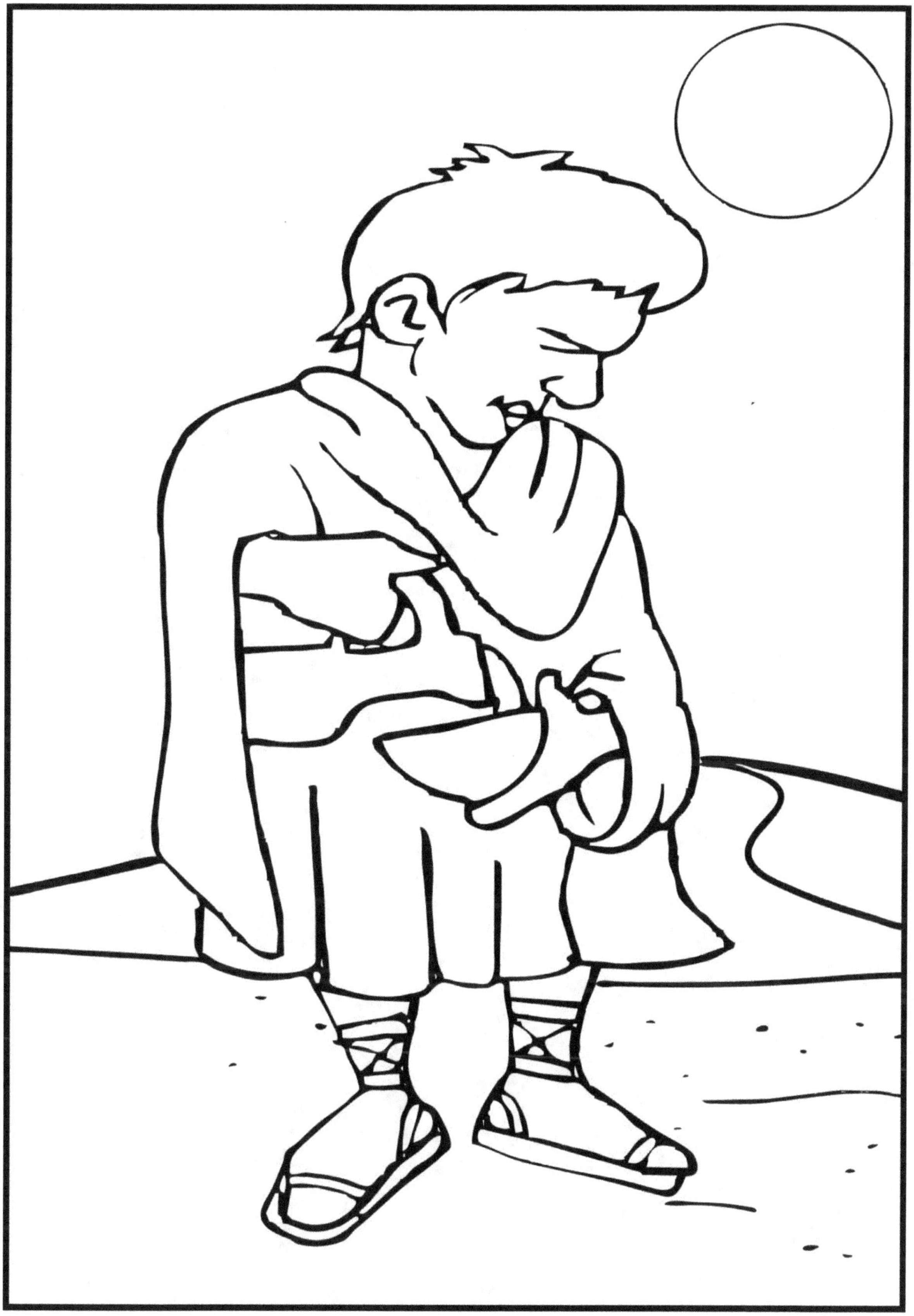

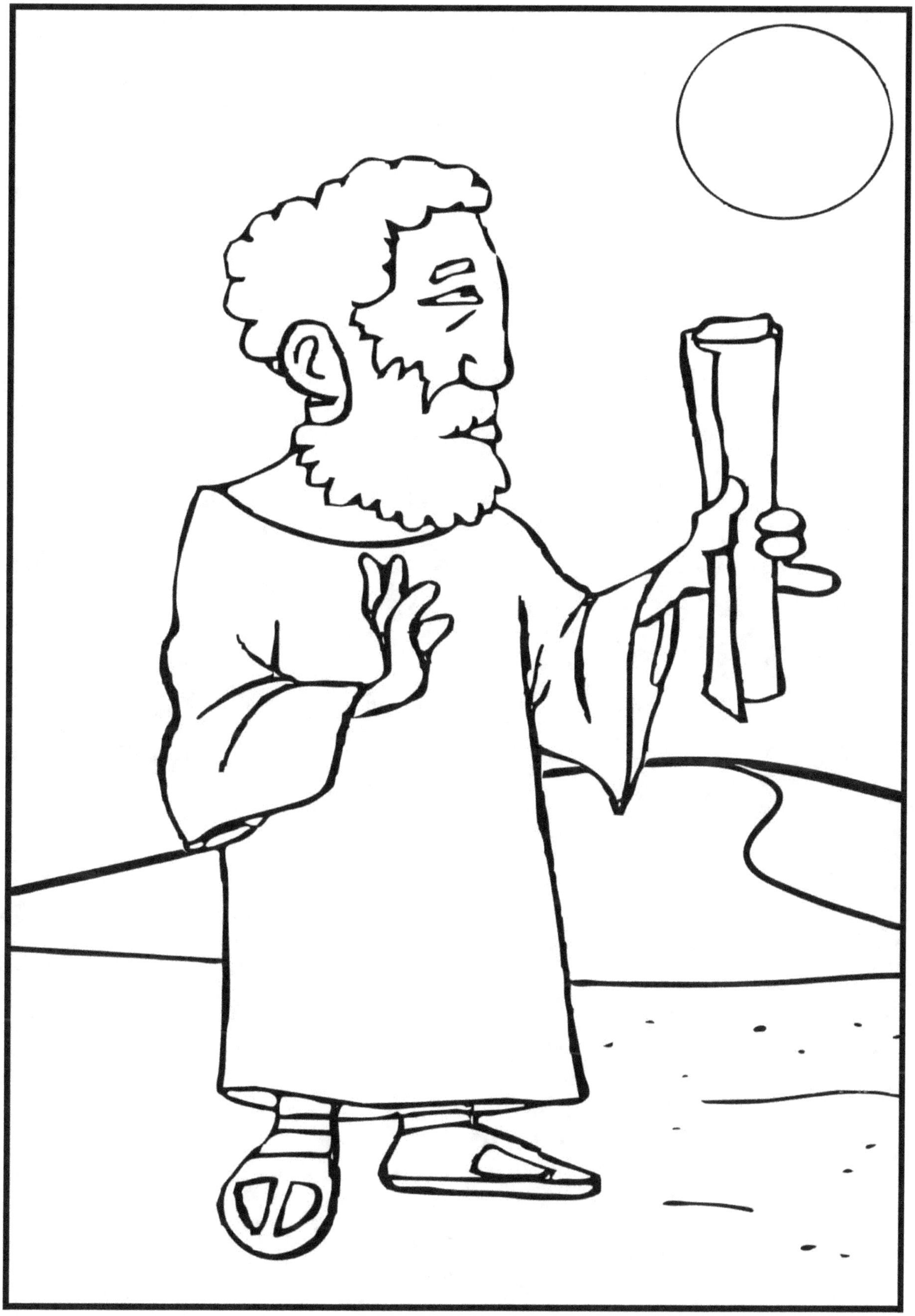

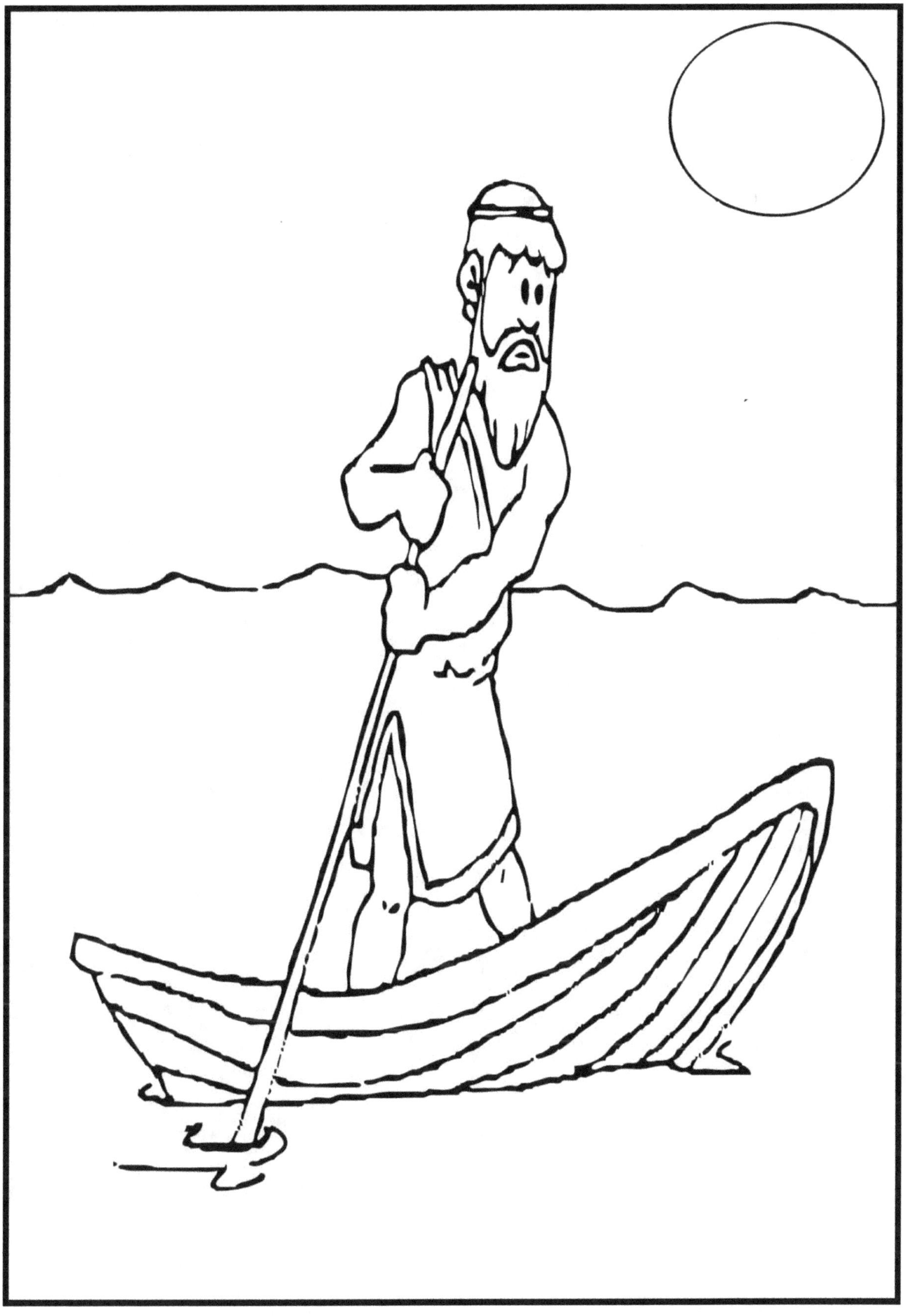

www.ingramcontent.com/pod-product-compliance
Lightning Source LLC
Chambersburg PA
CBHW081558170526
45166CB00009B/2736
* 9 7 8 1 5 2 2 7 2 6 8 9 0 *